Out There Somewhere

Volume 49

SVΠ TRACKS
An American Indian Literary Series

SERIES EDITOR
Ofelia Zepeda

EDITORIAL COMMITTEE
Vine Deloria, Jr.
Larry Evers
Joy Harjo
Geary Hobson
N. Scott Momaday
Irvin Morris
Simon J. Ortiz
Emory Sekaquaptewa
Kate Shanley
Leslie Marmon Silko
Luci Tapahonso

Out There Somewhere

SIMON J. ORTIZ

THE UNIVERSITY OF ARIZONA PRESS   TUCSON

The University of Arizona Press
© 2002 Simon J. Ortiz
All rights reserved

www.uapress.arizona.edu

Library of Congress Cataloging-in-Publication Data
Ortiz, Simon J., 1941–
Out there somewhere / Simon J. Ortiz.
p.   cm.—(Sun tracks ; v. 49)
ISBN 0-8165-2208-1 (acid-free paper)—
ISBN 0-8165-2210-3 (pbk. : acid-free paper)
1. Acoma Indians—Poetry. 2. New Mexico—Poetry.
I. Title. II. Series.
PS501.S85 vol. 49
[PS3565.R77]
810.8'0054 s—dc21
[811/.54]   2001002743

Publication of this book is made possible in part by
the proceeds of a permanent endowment created with
the assistance of a Challenge Grant from the National
Endowment for the Humanities, a federal agency.

Manufactured in the United States of America on acid-free,
archival-quality paper containing a minimum of 30% post-
consumer waste and processed chlorine free.

14   13   12   11   10   09   7   6   5   4   3   2

Contents

Preface

The title of this poetry and prose collection, *Out There Somewhere*, could be a translation of the Acoma phrase *hauchaw tyah haati*. It's a phrase spoken as a reply to a query by someone who is looking for another person, perhaps a parent looking for a child or a friend looking for his or her friend. Upon entering a room in a house, the parent or friend might ask, "Where is so-and-so?" And someone will reply, "Oh, he's out there somewhere," pointing outdoors, pointing beyond the house walls. With reference to this new collection of my poetry and prose, I've imagined the outdoors to be out there somewhere in everyday experience somewhere in America. I've spent a large part of my lifetime away from Acoma Pueblo—out there somewhere in America—away from the Acoma village area of Deetseyaamah where I grew up. But while I have physically been away from my home area, I have never been away in any absolute way. For many other Native people of the twentieth century and the beginning of the twenty-first, this has also been the case since many of us have lived away from our original homelands, cultures, and communities in one way or another. Yet at the same time that we are away, we also continue to be absolutely connected socially and culturally to our Native identity. We insist that we as human cultural beings must always have this connection because it is the way we maintain a Native sense of Existence.

Acknowledgments

I want to express heartfelt thanks to the Lannan Foundation for its artist residency program, which afforded me the time to complete this book. Although unrelated to the residency program, I wish also to commend the Lannan Foundation for its support of the self-development concerns of Native communities, especially regarding Native education and languages.

Thanks are also due Christine Szuter, Patti Hartmann, Alan M. Schroder, Ofelia Zepeda, and all of the staff of the University of Arizona Press and the Sun Tracks Series. And endless thanks to my children and grandchildren for their ongoing faith, support, and love.

The eight-part poem sequence "What Indians?" was featured at the Venice Biennale 1999–2000 as part of *Ceremonial*, a Native Arts Alliance exhibition. Some of the poems in this collection have appeared in *Red Ink, Ploughshares, ISLE, Sniper Logic, Writers' Forum, West Wind Review, Chokecherries 1998*, and the *South Dakota Review*. "Time as Memory as Story" was written for a Sharlot Hall Museum publication. Thanks to all.

PART ONE

MARGINS

The moon,
        the moon,
my voice in song.
To say
        to say
what I really mean to say.
Moon,
        moon song,
singing moon song.

Sitting outside the dining hall smoking. Anica, Emily, others. Emily offers a roll-your-own, which I decline.

I say, "In jail I've seen roll-your-owns so well made they're rolled better than machine-rolled ones." Nobody pays any mind.

Minutes earlier, Victor, Tanure, and I talk about prisons and reasons for people in jail. Victor from Mexico. Tanure from Nigeria. Me from Acoma. Drugs and alcohol, Victor says. Disadvantaged conditions, Tanure says. When I say Alaska has a 17 percent Native population in the state and a 70 percent Native inmate population in its state prisons, Victor shakes his head. Tanure nods yes, yes.

The moon, the moon, the best kind of sky is the sunset light of the Pacific Ocean. Suddenly I'm too lonesome again.

THURSDAY, JUNE 16, 9:56 A.M.
Shaky from the cold. Coming down the stairs from kitchenette above, a cup of instant coffee in one hand, a glass of orange juice in the other, almost feel like falling. And more than that. Yesterday morning while Tanure held a ladder for me as I replaced a light bulb, I felt a dizziness that feels like flying. You know what I mean? Not dizziness but flying. I think you'd fall into flight just like that.

I haven't shaved for three days. I like it.

Last night, three artists on tour from China ate with us. Two interpreters with them, one of them white. I asked the white one how he came to speak Chinese so fluently, which he seemed to do. "Because of the diplomatic corps," he said. I looked at him up and down and said to myself oh shit the fucking CIA. He was sent to school to learn Chinese he said. "At U.S. expense," he said. Kind of giggling, chuckling. Fucking CIA I thought, like I said.

One of the painters intense and interesting. Though I was kind of pissed when he said "it's limiting when artists define themselves within cultural restrictions." I said that Native American artists have been fighting five hundred years for their land, culture, and community.

One of those ways has been through art as a way of life and belief system. I said it was fortunate the Chinese were a majority in their own country, but here Indians are an oppressed minority in their own country!

The Chinese artist said there was current debate in China about the necessary distinctions of traditional cultural art.

I asked the other painter what knowledge there was of American Indian people in China. "Very little," he said, smiling. "Just the Western movies." I had to laugh. "Just like American knowledge of Indians in the U.S.," I said. They had not been able to visit any Indian reservations.

When I asked about the sponsor for their trip to the U.S., one painter said the U.S. government paid for the trip. How were the Chinese painters selected for the trip? someone asked. "There was a competition held by 3M Corporation" was the reply. Okay. Government and business. Government business.

I suggested the reason the artists had not visited Indian reservations to talk with traditional cultural artists was because they were not permitted to do so by their tour sponsor. The white tour guide and the other translator said that couldn't possibly be the reason!

I miss Kelly. Ah, Kelly, sweet Irish Cherokee, serious and frightened eyes. Holding, holding. Afraid to be hurt by me or anyone else. Rock and roll and country guitar. Geesus, Kelly, how could you love such a selfish self-centered fool like me? At the rehab center session you with your best clothes on. I knew they were, I knew you treasured them. Your face trembly and shaky, eyes teary. You just held on and held on. At that point you would have done anything but save me. Because I didn't want to be saved. Saying I love you softly I love you silently your lips barely moving, holding one last time. . . .

So today I decided to take my chest cold to the sea coast and the sea wind.

At one point high above the ocean, I climbed a trail along a narrow, sandy rock ledge, which at first I had turned away from. And then with a quick flip of the mind, I turned back. Said okay I'll go ahead and climb it. With a kind of don't give a damn mind. Geesus, that's what's gotten me in jams before! I even thought of the dizziness I felt yesterday. The feeling of suddenly gliding away, somewhere toward somewhere.

From atop the Headlands granite ridges and bluffs overlooking the Bay toward San Francisco. Hundreds of feet below, the Pacific surf surging and roaring upon ragged rocks. A giddy headiness—I'm thinking I hadn't taken my medication last night. I went on ahead, scampering and leaning into the steep incline on the narrow slippery trail.

On flatter, safer ground seventy yards away I looked back, and I couldn't believe it. My breath letting out, a rubbery weakness trembling me. I'm shaky too. But feeling an odd gentle loving feeling. What is it? I don't know. It's like I'm going to fly toward somewhere. It will suddenly not be dizziness anymore but a sudden release of energy that is flight.

Jog for the first time in a long time. Raggy chest from too much smoking. But no smoking now. I can feel sense of smell returning. Smoke in clothes, neckerchief.

Jog on asphalt trail to the lighthouse. Turn at the road where a Nike missile sat yesterday in the parking lot. What? A dummy or a real one? Yeah. I don't know. Yesterday? Yeah. A silo port built into the hill behind it. Around the Nike were families imagining the missile lifting off. Fire, smoke, immense thunder. At twenty I was with a Hawk missile unit at Fort Bliss. Our unit would go to White Sands Missile Range.

It used to be a thrill seeing Hawk missiles launching from their pads. Crazy. Insane. Madness. Geesus. Partly fear, partly something else. Thrill = adrenaline + no brains.

Feels good to jog on the beach. Count paces. Three hundred at a time. Half a mile or so. Be careful. You have limits. You're fifty-three now.

Happy Father's Day card from Sara yesterday. Love and thank you. She's twelve. Happy Daughter's Day to you.

Last day of spring. Tomorrow the first day of summer.

Said to Lauri, Headlands Arts Center cook, I would put her cooking in my journal. As the cook, she's the true and real artist here. The rest of us are just writers, painters, dancers, though we do wash dishes and clean up things pretty good after we eat the food Lauri cooks! Art is food: delicious shrimp, salad goulash (fresh corn, green beans, onions, cucumbers), garlic bread, wild rice. And pastry shortbread with raspberry sauce and peaches and cream. Delicious and delightful.

And a long talk with Kentucky, who's from Louisville, a city where I arrived one night drunk.

Got up in the impossible morning, I told Kentucky, stumbled downstairs into the conference hotel lobby full of professors in their professor suits and dresses. What the hell was I doing there? I have no idea except I'm to give a workshop talk at 8:30. A hopeless alcoholic paranoia and panic grips me. I can't drink in the hotel bar so I stumble into the street. Thinking this is where Muhammad Ali grew up as a street kid named Cassius Clay. Somehow that makes me feel safe or something although the Louisville streets are reeling gray and nauseously around me. I need a drink, geesus, I pray. Praying, for crissakes.

Kentucky intensely studied my face.

And my prayers were answered at the corner, a downstairs dive bar, smelly and dark, dangerous maybe, probably, but I didn't care, I just needed a drink real bad. So I stumbled down the stairs and ordered a vodka, just vodka. Make it a double I said. Shaky and absolutely crazed by then. Three tired-looking old white guys look at me, one of them wags his head at me. I ask for tomato juice then, which the bartender doesn't have so I have grapefruit. And another vodka which takes all my strength to keep down. I look at the dirty floor and shake my head after I swallow the shit. Geesus, that was Louisville, yes.

Kentucky looked at me for a long moment when I finished my story. And I think she almost wagged her head like the old guy.

WEDNESDAY, JUNE 29, 11:20 P.M.

Baked salmon, new potatoes, green salad tonite. Great stuff.

SATURDAY, JULY 2, 7:45 P.M.

It doesn't do any good just to hang around feeling shitty.

Yet that's what I was doing all day long. And nothing to show for it. Nothing.

So I decided to go to the beach. Watch the sunset.

Where is the poetry?
At the beach.
Who took it there?
It's always been there.
Just there?
Yeah, just there.

Little stones. Little stones. Seagulls. Gray shiny water. Silver and gold flashes.
March. I think it was March. Ocean Isle, North Carolina. Warm then, not lonely.
Stones and foamy water. The Atlantic. Pacific here. The fog this morning too.

The poetry at the beach was always there. The poetry at the beach was sharp light.

TUESDAY, JULY 12, 3:45 P.M.

Hold out your hand, I say to Cynthia.
When I walk up holding out folded sheets of paper.
And the stones and shells in my hand.
She smiles. But doesn't hold out her hands.
Instead she withdraws them, holds them back.
Tiny hands. Open your hands, I say.
What is it? she asks. Don't ask, don't be afraid.
But what is it? she asks. Just open your hands
And receive what's real. Art. Stones. Shells.

THURSDAY, JULY 14, 10:07 A.M.

Talk about risk last night. Headlands Center for the Arts is located within federal property managed by the U.S. Park Service and its bureaucratic rules. Which requires Headlands Center artists to abide by the rules. Risk by the rules?

Renee is Mexican Indian, dark skinned.
I'm risking my reputation, he says.

And he says about another artist's work,
That's not risk, that's business!
What did your people gain, Indian?
What did your people lose, Indian?
What is risk? Is there any such thing as risk at all?
The question is asked by a Chinese artist with bright inquisitive eyes.

Good question.

No. There is nothing at risk.
There is nothing at risk in this fucked up nation and epoch.
THEY got it all. And they don't have to risk.
THEY want us to risk. But for THEM, there is no risk.

Unless we push the matter forward. Risk.

What would happen if we put up signs saying NO ENTRY. PRIVATE
  PROPERTY.

Signs which stated **U.S. GOVERNMENT STAY OUT.**

Signs which state

ATTENTION LIARS, THIEVES, AND KILLERS

You have stolen enough land and life.
From here on out, you are no longer allowed access.
We claim back our land and life.
Go away.
Do not enter.

You think that will shake them?
You would think so.
But I don't know. Maybe. But it has to be approved by the U.S. Park
Service.
Memo: No risks allowed without proper clearance and authorization by
the U.S. Government. Please come to the office for approval. Immediately.

No. Just a sign will do:

This land is no longer yours.
We are taking back what is ours.
It was never yours.
Please leave.

Would that be risk?
It would probably get some attention, but would it be risk?

White people especially, please note.
We know there are some good guys among you,
but there are some absolutely bad ones
who are everywhere.
We mean some real shitheads. No, more serious than that.
Killers, thieves, liars to the max.
The ones who built those missile silo bunkers on the hills,
the ones who brought in the Nikes
and display one disarmed (?) every Sunday, 12:30–5:30 P.M.,
the ones who hide downtown in the bank buildings
or live in Tiburon or are taking Paris summer vacations,
those ones, those white people,
the scary ones, please note.

I wrote a poem some time ago. What was the last line in it? "s/Sinagua
Indians / SEE MUSEUM FOR MORE INFORMATION."

Risk has to be more than personal risk. It has to concern itself with ethical,
moral, political, social, historical, spiritual, material issues and questions.
Personal risk is the least at stake.

Life is at stake.

Walking a tightrope. And falling or not falling. Crucifixion. Car racing.
Jumping out of airplanes. Putting stuff in a computer memory and hoping
it'll be there again next time you open up the machine. Spilling your
guts out to someone else. Telling someone you love them or not telling
someone you love them. Those are important risks but they're selfish and
self-centered stuff mainly.

NO RISKS ALLOWED
UNLESS AUTHORIZED
BY THE AMERICAN WAY
OF LIFE AND THE U.S. GOVERNMENT
(On your way out, please contribute $$$.
It costs $$ to run your lives.
U.S. $ only.)

SUNDAY, JULY 24, 11:15 A.M.

It's kinda crazy when I think about it.

I shouldn't get into situations like this I thought. I might kill somebody. Or get killed.

The man, Michael, spoke from the backseat. "It's good for them to hear you speak in a foreign language. A language they don't know, y'know."

I didn't know what to say, so I didn't say anything right away.

Until somehow I managed to say, "You mean the Acoma Pueblo language I was speaking."

"Yeah," he said from the backseat. "That language. The foreign one."

Sometimes I feel like killing somebody.

After poetry readings though, most times, usually, people are polite. And they say thank you, sometimes referring to something I brought up in poetry.

This time I overheard a tall, blonde, freckled woman with broad shoulders and an intense manner say, "Indians are hard to save."

Before and Behind Me

JANUARY 28, 1987

I look in the mirror.
Before me is a brown face,
strained, thinner
than five years ago.
Behind me is a tilted lamp shade.
Orange light.
A large, cheap chest of drawers.
A chair with two towels, jeans draped.
A box of unrelated, unresolved papers.
Letters, documents, forms.
   No poems.
   No stories.
Just the words I've written from habit.
   A dime on the night stand.
   Ashtray which I keep emptying.
A single room key and not much more.
   There has been more than this.
Late at night,
early, early in the morning.
   There are poems.
   There are stories.
Before me in the mirror.
Behind me in the mirror.

Transcribing

The act is to remember
without losing the moment.
It was the cheap hotel room
in the Tenderloin, third floor.
Thumps in the ceiling,
clumsy calls for help
in the walls; night, night.
To remember the minutes
without losing the present.
More precious than now,
as it was then, now
more than any other time
the imperative not to lose.

Essentialism

Knowing about being Indian
just because
you're an Indian.

What?
            Hunh?
        Huh?
Say something?

                                    No one knows
                                    about being white,
                                    just like no one knows
                                    about being Indian.
                    Or Latino.
                    Or black.
                    Or Martian.

But I do know more about being Indian
than being white or Latino or black or Martian.

And that means
I do know more about being Indian
than you do.

Have you ever heard anyone ask what does it feel like to be white?

And what do you feel when you're asked too frequently about being
Indian, Latino, or black?

What does it feel like to be Indian?

Really, I want to know.

Seriously?

Is essentialism untenable? Or is essentialism tenable?

I don't know everything about myself as an Indian but I do know a few things about it. That's the best I can do, believe me. I'm not bullshitting you.

man sometimes i feel like punching someone out or even killing it's so crazy you know you just feel like it when you get those stupid ass questions like some kind of test not that they're even serious queries but feel more like deliberate harassing and demeaning ones that get you so riled you squirm and fidget and think insane twisted thoughts your emotions tangling and twisting your face and making you swallow hard

History's Midst

After the Thursday AA meeting, I walk.
Down to the BART stop on Powell, I walk.
For a couple of minutes I listen
to a street pianist. Jazz rock.
Jazz rock Christmas carols mingling
with the street noise, night traffic
and city chaos, loud talk and sirens.

A man preaches of the Lord's coming.
You better know this is the Lord's history.
Close by another man sells trinkets—
baubles and beads, plastic and stones—
which glitter in the wintery sunlight.

I know there are things to say
about all this—city, traffic, people
bumping into each other, trinkets,
jazz rock, Christmas—and myself caught
in the midst of my own history, but for now
all I can say to the piano man and his music
is, "Thanks for your music, man," silently.
And turn to the trinket man and say,
"Nice, nice," gently touch a ring inlaid
with abalone shell, and say again, "Nice."

The Lord's preacher is street stern
and strident at my back as I leave.
He's sure of it, and I'm sure of it too.
It is time and not too soon nor too late.
A child again will be born into the midst
of history, his and your history, our history.

Hoping to Hear

Someone knocking.
Knocking, knocking.
On the vent above my jail bunk.

Unseen voice, voice.

An urgent appeal,
an unquiet conspiracy
trying to raise life from within
the unlife
of these walls.

Knocking,
knocking.
Knocking.

Like a sick heart.
Or a weakened
and wobbly knee.

Desperation grown small, stunted.
Begging,
pathetic.

Urgently, urgently seeking,
hoping to hear
assurance
from a farther above
or even a further below.
From anywhere.
Just as long as something returns.
Anything.

Chant

I dozed off after finishing *Man's Fate*. What better thing to do? Doze off.
After waking time has passed but what of it? I look out the slit-narrow
county jail window. I see evening light is different from midday light
but that has nothing to do with time. What does time have to do with
anything?

> 7 P.M. Now is my reality.
> The reality is now.
> My reality is now.
> Now is my reality.

I've been chanting silently
in the frustrating moments
before I have finally slept.
The chant is a formula
to drive away fantasy
that is either repressive
or futuristic.
I've discovered and decided
that fantasy is a distraction
and a diversion useful only
for avoiding reality.

> Now is my reality.
> The reality is now.
> My reality is now.
> Now is my reality. 7:30 P.M.

"Be a good Buddhist," says Carol the jailhouse psychologist.
Smiling, I tell her I am really Alan Watts.
I've been reading *In My Own Way*.
"I know better," she says and smiles back.

BE

Be a good Buddhist.
Be a good Buddhist in jail.

I wake up strangely.
A bright, bright light penetrating everything.
A feeling like I'm someplace far from here.
A feeling like I'm in a hiding place.
A feeling like I'm in a sanatorium.
A feeling that my body and mind are separate.
Two places. Two people.

I try to rejoin them.
I try, I try, I try so hard I even grunt with the effort.

Finally it happens.

Because I made a decision to have no breakfast.
To have no breakfast is a kind of freedom. Yeah.
To have no breakfast.

If not a good Buddhist, then a smiling Buddhist.

Later I awake again.
And I'm late. I can tell I am.
I'm groggy, my movement slow, cumbersome.
Slowly I make my bed, go shit, wipe.
Then I fumble with the toothpaste and start to brush my teeth.
Cumbersome and slow, cumbersome and slow.
Then I stop everything because the jail intercom says my name.

I'm taken down to the infirmary.
The nurse tells me she's in a hurry
as she changes the dressing on my hand.

It's okay I say just as long as it's changed.
It's shift change. Things are adrift.
            We get into a discussion
about the stitches in my thumb.
It's obvious they should come out.
When the doctor comes and says
let's take them out, I say okay let's do it.
Snip, snip, simple little twitches
of the scissors and tweezers, snip, snip.
Little tendril roots of quick pain,
nothing else, and it's done.
            There's pain only upon twisting and bending.
            Only upon twisting and bending, there's pain.

Be: twisting and bending: pain.

            Be a good Buddhist without smiling.

In the Moment Before

As he prayed, he thought:
the land, the way of life, the community.
Ours. Our own. Our heart, blood, soul.
Yours, the grandmothers and grandfathers said.
Yours, ours, yours, ours, always, always.

As he thought, he prayed:
always this is ours, our way of life,
this is why we must fight for ourselves, always.

And today, we must think as we pray:
always one with our struggle, hope, and continuance,
always for the sake of the land, culture, and community.

For Now It's Enough: Late Night at ARA House: Thank God

After midnight. What else can a late night be but late. A question and not a question. Not much to know, not sleepy though tired. A dull taste in the mouth, and a tugging or pushing at something—something from within, from inside. Not quite sure what it is, nerves or something. Something. Not even remembering other late nights. Maybe a security in not remembering, a security in not knowing anything for sure.

It's okay not to remember as long as I don't expect anything. From time to time it's okay. Worry some other time. Or let others worry about what I'm supposed to be doing. I'm just glad I'm alive, just glad I'm not dead. Like Jim Pepper sings in his song. Just glad I've been looking forward to today. And that I've been sober to this point. It's 12:39 A.M., and I've made it this far. Yesterday is gone, I didn't drink, and I'm glad.

For that gladness, be thankful. Be happy. That's what I tell myself. But shit I didn't do much today. And shitty job I've done tonight. Not much happened, answered the phone several times, sat down to write to Peg. Old love, want to talk with her, hold her, love her, that's all, not much. But more than I have right now, more than possible perhaps. Though anything may happen anytime, again. Give it time. No it won't. Give it time anyway. It's all right I have only these feelings and not much more than that.

Be glad you're thankful for being glad. Thank God you're not dead.

Put out 9:30 P.M. snacks. Not much there either. Cheese, bagels, stale white bread, peanut butter and jam. Slice off moldy cheese edge. And bread pudding. That's all. Put coffee on. Nobody touches much of anything. Cook made the bread pudding and served it at supper. Nobody touched it then. Nobody touched it tonight. It's that way with everything. There just isn't much happening. There's just not much to expect. Thank God you're not dead.

I'm glad that's all there is, these measly little things. If there were more, I don't know what I'd do. I'd have to make choices, take chances, decide, and I really don't want to do that tonight.

For now, my life is enough. There's not much more to expect. I laid down on my bed for a while this afternoon after I got back from Oakland and started to take a short nap. But then I wanted to run. Just run. So I put on my jogging outfit and shoes but by the time I was ready to go out it started to rain. So I didn't run much, just down the hill to the drugstore and got some envelopes I've been meaning to get for several days. It was cold out too and I wanted to run for just a bit, not far, just a bit farther. But that was okay too. It's like everything else. I don't want a lot. Just enough.

Seed

I.
He looked at the seed for a long time.
His mind did not comprehend.
It did not flower anymore.
The seed was just a seed.

She had said it was begonia.
He tried to imagine what begonias looked like.
Purple blossoms, rich yellow, supple orange, blue petals?

The mind that made the seed bloom was always the poet.

He was not the poet anymore.

II.
When he decided to give up poetry,
it was one o'clock in the afternoon.
It was a Tuesday, and he stood in the middle of a corridor
trying to think of where to go, where he was to be.
Where? he wondered. Mighty big question, he decided.
He knew then he would quit trying to write poetry,
the seed he thought he carried with him all his life.
Here he was at forty-five years old still trying
to show he was the one who would show
such life in images no one could deny.

There were no images.
He watched his graduate seminar students stumbling
into H-103 every Tuesday afternoon.
The Grim Section they called it, Richard's class,
the one with the dark side of Tennyson.
Tennyson had no major dark side, not a grim one anyway,
but he brought it out. He made sure of it.

It wasn't true, but he made it true.
There were no such images, he thought.

So at one o'clock on a Tuesday afternoon,
Richard decided, No more.
He didn't say anything to the blonde female student
walking straight up to him as he turned away.
He could have walked through walls, ether walls,
and star-sheened walls, and even solid walls
when he left Hallmer Hall without looking back.

III.
When he reached First Elk River,
the stream of water was not like any he had ever stood by.
Not even the one he had created when his parents,
professors, and wives had said, You are the gentlest,
subtlest, most sincere one.
                              Sure he took advantage
of the Buddha when he said, Why not.
                                        And laughed,
and they smiled and said to others, That's what he says.

Now by First Elk River all he could see were reeds
and the water flowing.
Unsteadily he was the angle of water turning.
And he remembered one of his lectures at the beginning
of the semester when he had brought up a Chinese poet
who observed that nothing turns without meaning to.
Unsteadily he was turning but now he was meaning to turn.

IV.
There was a story he liked that no one else remembered.
It was a funeral story by an Irish writer, he was sure.
Maybe the writer who wrote *A Tree Grows in Brooklyn*.
Someone who had said, "No one ever sees the river anymore."
Maybe he made that up; he couldn't remember either anymore.

They had not forgotten, but it was best to forget,
so they forgot.
          But the fishing they didn't forget;
at least the memory of fishing they didn't forget.
So he remembered the flowing current as he watched
the trout swim deftly through the current shifting always.

He did not want to be a poet anymore.
He did not want to be swayed by the lilt of a bird somewhere
beyond his view as he reached his hand toward the current
shifting everything away, and he did not want to know
the seed that stood before his eyes as a tiny monument
of new life, the beginning that would flower by his seeing.

Пот ву Any Chance

The corner of Burnside and Union is not the edge of the world. Car traffic,
streetlight flash, the invisible siren wail every short hour. It's Portland.

"Man, the woods are the place to be," Tom says. "Cutting trees. Up
there in Tulalip, Indians, the air smelling of smoke." He takes a deep shaky
breath.

I'm silent. Not thinking too hard. It's too hard to think in the detox
haze.

The TV is pretty loud down the hall and the dudes and women are
talking just as loud or louder. They're all right though, just wiggy. One or
two of them tweaking. Not bad if you don't have to be here. This is not
the edge of the world, just the damn outside of it.

The only quiet place is the little alcove.

I recall the little mountain alcove upriver from Eureka. Nothing but
woods. Far from the corner that's frenzied city light and frenzied night.

"Once I got a deer near Klamath," Tom says. "I didn't know what to do
with it. So I said to Quickman this big Indian, What now?"

Tom turns his head toward me to make sure I'm listening which I am
sort of. Then he says, "Quickman kinda laughed but didn't say nothing.
And then he took out his big K-bar. And looked at me."

Tom stops talking, like he's stuck in the shadow of a thought for a
moment.

And then he says, "Quickman ran his big thumb along the blade edge
and shrugged his shoulder at me. Man, I felt a cold shudder run deep
up my elbow to my shoulder. It was the deer or me I thought. And then
Quickman started on the deer."

This place is not very far away. In my life I've been barely alive once or twice and I've been pretty damn close to my real last chance.

The alcove protects me though and the alcove protects the others too. Here at Hooper Memorial Center—sounds like a mortuary but it's actually a detox—we give ourselves the chance we've always deserved.

The street outside is running with winey puke, sour sweat, bloody men and women.
I see this out the smudged window.
I hear the mournful wail of a ghost hiding from the dense heart of the city.
And through the screened window drifts the smell of Indian woods and smoke.

The Spring

He told her what he was going to do.

What else is new? she said.

She finished putting the winter jumper on the baby. She kissed and
  hugged her.

He stood there like he stood at the corner of the world.

I told you, she said, what you do is your business. You don't have any
  here.

He held out his trembly hand to the baby.

The baby looked at it like she might look at cold chicken.

Baby, he said weakly.

Uummgh, the baby said, and she hugged her mother.

There wasn't much on the other side of his fate except the usual
  wreckage.

Go on, he said again. She's probably there. She'll tell you.

I know what she'll say. The usual shit. Go to hell, she said. Right now.

Go hell, the baby said.

There wasn't anything to say anymore.

Might as well talk to the fucking sky.

He tried one more time though. What are you going to do? he said.

She didn't hesitate. I'll call the fucking cops if you don't leave right now, she said.

Rye now, the baby said.

His head spun down from the larger circle.

The spiral became small. Then smaller and tight. Like a spring.

Please don't do that, he said. His voice quavered. Please just listen.

He felt like the coiled spring was in his hand.

It made his whole arm tremble.

The baby was now fully dressed and mother and child moved toward the door.

Please leave, he heard his ex-wife say.

You must try, the counselor had said. Forgive yourself.

He had tried and he had tried and he had failed every task.

Keep a journal, the counselor had said. Do your fourth step.

Talk to your sponsor, keep talking, go to meetings, make amends.

He had tried and then he had not tried.

Keep failing, keep failing, and finally you will have what you do not.

Finally you will have what you do not have.

The end of the world will be yours.

When the police came, he stood outside the door. The spring loaded and ready.

It Didn't Matter

I don't even recall what they called the patrol that roamed Market Street, the Mission, and the Tenderloin.

Harwood. Hopewood? Hopeful? Hellbound? Hell Patrol? I don't remember. And I didn't really care.

Now?

I want to remember I must never be there again. Never. I swear, I swear. (Even though you're never to say never!)

You ended up where they took you.

They put me in the paddy. Shackled me to a metal cot or something. The universe shaky all around.

I might as well have been in hell or on the way there.

Like I said I didn't really care. It didn't matter.

My head down seemed to be the only way to hold it. Insides churning black and ugly, the world spinning with the crazies.

Crazies? Besides mine, there were some real ones in that hellish haven in the Mission.

Sitting around and talking loud, so loud your head can't really take it but does because there is no choice.

Getting ferociously sick and going into the filthy toilet where you're prepared for anything. Anything.

But I could hardly stand, just kind of prop my wobbly self against the graffiti wall and piss. And look at what I had made my world into.

The questions the social worker asked—I guess she was hell's social worker: Where are you from? Where do you work? Next of kin? Do you have any money?

Fuck, I didn't know. And I couldn't remember. It didn't make a difference anyway—why should it?

All I felt was sick, sick, sick.

My deathly sick bones were tubes of jello. My world inside was a garbage pit and burnt-down buildings. What was left of my mind was thinking evil things.

It didn't matter what evil things; everything was evil to me.

I was at the end of the world. But it didn't matter; it was only San Francisco.

PART TWO

IMAGES

"Beiⴖɢ Poor" ⴖⴖⴅ Powerless. ⴖⴖⴅ Refusiⴖɢ Aɢaiⴖ

Roxanne calls and says, "Guess who's back in town?"

I don't know. I try to think back twenty years ago or so. 1976, 1977. But I don't know. OK, who?

"Mendoza."

A surprise sort of, but then maybe not.

"There was a story in the newspaper about him living in a shack some-where in the East Bay. He talked about being very poor. So he's still at it," she says. And adds without any sympathy, "He reminds me of my father."

I think of myself. Being poor, feeling mostly powerless because of it. I know, I know, poverty doesn't have to mean powerlessness. Yet that's how it mostly is.

I think of the Unabomber's letter to a Mexican peasant farmer, telling him he had $53.01 to last him through the hard Montana winter.

And I think of myself at times counting my last pennies again. Feeling poor. Feeling poor again and again yet at the same time also refusing poverty I think.

I don't know though. I'm still at it too. Refusing. Again.

I know too well the powerlessness that poverty eventually becomes.

And when I think of it again I wonder how many of us have made plans for bombs intended for corporations, their banks, and the police state that protects them from the poor and the powerless.

Anthropology of American Scholars: Notes, That Is

What?

Two women stand to "give their papers"

and

one man sits to read his.

Why?

The man asks, "Why do people say they have a special bond to land?"

Ethnicity and territory coincide perfectly.

"They carved farms out of wilderness."

Form and style.

"Style is a matter of preference," I wrote once in a poem.

"Myth of form as the proper place."

What? Why? What in the world does that mean?

Need permit to travel from Cape Town.

Idea of "proper" for her *somewhere*.

Without a doubt there is a homeland *somewhere*.

Africa
America
African natives

American natives

Homeland somewhere
Homeland somewhere

Refugees from war.

After the war, did they go home? If they did, where was home?

"Transcendental justification for land ownership."

What? Why? They didn't need any. They just took the land and became owners!

Making deserted land bloom. Assures cultivation of land. Cultivation and nervous tension go hand in hand.

Form versus Wilderness.

"I am becoming a different kind of man." Me too.

Construction of the unconstructed. Me too.

Rights of cultivators take precedence over nomads!

Read: Whites' contribution to civilizing of South Africa.

Read: Whites' contribution to civilizing of the Americas.

Read: Natives' contribution to civilizing of Whites.

After the session, I have to take a break from listening and taking notes and wondering. So I leave the conference center and walk across the parking lot to a grassy hill sloping down to a murky river. Across the river is a stand of trees and a paved path through the trees. I want to cross the river and walk along the path into the trees. But there is no way to cross the river, and so I'm stuck with more listening and taking notes and wondering.

Back East. But When? Where? What? Who?

It was right there. Yet peripheral. But right before him.
A list of places, names of places where he'd been.
But when? 1980? Yes, he agreed with himself silently
after studying the list.
                    Yet he could not
quite remember, couldn't place the moments,
the details.
                    That was ten years ago he thought.
Ten years. Ten years since he'd been back east.

He remembered The Gallery somewhere. But where?
Actually outside The Gallery talking with somebody.

But who? Several people. But who were they?

They had just met and he did not know them.
Or is it that he doesn't remember who they were?
They had invited him for a drink next door
but he didn't go with them.
                    No, he said, but thanks.
He remembered that very clearly, saying that.

I should have gone with them he thought now.
Maybe I'd remember who they were. And where.
And what happened, all the details, everything.

He didn't even remember his poetry reading.
There is more than just people to remember,
he thought now. There's always lots to remember.
What the hell took place anyway and where?
Where the hell was The Gallery anyway? New York?

He wasn't drinking that time. In fact that period
of his life was without drinking for a good while.

And

it bothered him even more he didn't remember when,
where, what the hell took place, and who was there.

39

A blackout he could understand or at least accept
but loss of memory while stone sober bothered him.

So

it's peripheral, accept it, he thought, it's peripheral, accept it.

Histories, Places, Indians, Just Like Always

FREIBURG, GERMANY, JUNE 1992

Near the hotel I'm at, a Quechua Indian group plays music.
Incas, I say to myself. Flutes, stringed instruments, a violin.
Andean music. Peru, I say in a whisper.
Crossing the street to say hello, I see they have a bit
of change, some deutsche marks in a little box.
A woman, three men, dark skin, smiling hard,
listening hard to their music. Far from home, I say quietly.

NEW YORK CITY, NEW YORK, DECEMBER 1992

Walking back to the MLA conference,
I see a man with a scribbled sign saying Need Money
To Get Back Home to Window Rock, Navajo Nation.
I approach him, say, "Yaahteh," holding out my hand, smiling.
The 42nd Street traffic up and down the street is ceaseless.
The man looks at me, shakes his head and ignores my hand.

MARTINIQUE, FRENCH WEST INDIES, MARCH 1993

Veronique, Yannick, and Lydie show me Saint-Pierre.
In 1902, Mount Pelée erupted, its volcanic explosion
wiping out 30,000 French colonialists, only one African survived.
On the way to Saint-Pierre, Veronique says to me,
"There's a magic-mystic tree in Martinique that never dies.
It's called Acoma, spelled exactly like you spell Acoma.
Even when it's chopped down its center core stays green and alive.
It will grow again many years later. It never dies. It keeps living."

FROSTBURG, MARYLAND, APRIL 1993

After the Cumberland FM rock music station interview,
MaGuire and I walk to the historic local museum.
Historic railroad station, historic canal, historic town

where George Washington slept one night, historic postcards.
Noticing no Indians anywhere, I ask a clerk in the museum shop,
"Who are the Indians native to western Maryland?"
Looking puzzled, the clerk shrugs and shows me a book
that refers briefly to Indians on one or two pages.

SANTA FE, NEW MEXICO, JULY 1993

A Pueblo Indian man talks about taxes, Indians, culture, and art.
Until the portal was wrecked lately by a Santa Fe teenager,
he sold shell jewelry daily under the Governor's Palace portal.
"I don't know when they'll let us sell there again.
Maybe when they tell us. If they let us. Just like always.
Now there's the tax threat again. Again, just like always.
Going and coming, they threat us again, you know.
The land and now our culture and art too, just like always," he says.

The Law

1ST ONE
Hey, there's a law you know!
    What law you talking about?
No Indians Allowed.
    I ain't no Indian. I'm Mexican.
No Mexicans allowed either.
    Oh that law is an old one.

2ND ONE
Hey, there's a law you know!
    What law you talking about?
No Mexicans allowed.
    I ain't no Mexican. I'm Indian.
No Indians allowed either.
    Oh that law is an old one.

CONCLUSION
It's the same old law, the same one
we're gonna break no matter what.

Welcome to America the Mall

This is the Mall.

Call Jewelers
Eddie Bauer
Mervyns
GUESS
Dillards
Wicks 'n' Sticks
SoftWare Etc.
Bath & Body Works
Lilia Rubin
Broadway
VGI

And Etc. and Etc.

This is America. This is where you buy it.

What did my old white friend Peg say?

"I'm glad my children are not consumer oriented."

I'm glad also.
But it pisses me off she can say that.
That she should say that.
With no compunction about it.
That she and her children can afford
not to be consumer oriented.

Protected by privilege.
Because they're within it.
They have the protection of a consumer culture.
Because they're within it.

Strange. But not strange.

This is America where poor people have to pay for bare survival.

This is the Mall.
Welcome.
Because we're within it.

WHAT INDIANS?

The Truth Is: "No kidding?" "No." "Come on! That can't be true!" "No kidding."

"What Indians?" is my too-often unspoken response to people who ask "When do the Indians dance?" Like other colonized Indigenous peoples, cultures, and communities throughout the world, Native Americans have experienced and endured identities imposed upon them by colonial powers, most of which originated in Europe. This imposition has resulted to a great extent—more than we admit and realize—in the loss of a sense of a centered human self and the weakening and loss of Indigenous cultural identity.

Strange

April 9, 1999, 9:15 A.M.
Snow in soft wet knots
falling,
coming down
through gray trees.

        Strange to think of Iowa and Kansas.
        And Washington where I've never been in winter.
        And Portland, Oregon, where I've lived
        —elms and pines dripping with rain
        on Umatilla Street in weather like this—
Sellwood Bridge
over the Willamette River.

Strange . . .
        Nebraska, South Dakota, elsewhere . . .

But this is Salt Lake City, Utah.

Yeah, it could be elsewhere. In fact,
> it could be Somewhere Else City,
> United States of America, Planet Earth,
> but this is Salt Lake City
> right smack on the western edge
> of the center of the world, believe it or not.

Yeah, it's not elsewhere. It's not Somewhere Else City. It is

Salt Lake City
Salt Lake City
Salt Lake City
Salt Lake City
Salt Lake City

No where else but.
And, yeah, what a place, what a place.

What a place to think of Indians.

"Where are the Indians?"
"What Indians?"
"You know, Indians."
"I don't know what you're talking about."

Greatest Believers Greatest Disbelievers

To believe or not to believe,

this was the question.
And THE ANSWER.

Asked and answered and believed
by the greatest believers
and disbelievers the world has ever known.

Where are the Indians?
Where are the real Indians?

There are no Indians.
There are no real Indians.

There were never any Indians.
There were never any Indians.

There were never any real Indians.

You mean . . . you mean, there were never any Indians? No real Indians?
  No Indians?

None.
Never.

Real or unreal.
Real and/or unreal.
They were made up.
It didn't matter.

They were what people in Europe believed.
They were what people in Europe wanted:
to believe.
They were what people in Europe wanted.
`To believe.

Indians were what people in Europe wanted to believe. Indians were what people in Europe wanted to believe. Indians were what people in Europe wanted to believe.

"Indians" were what people in Europe wanted to believe.

"Indians" were what Europeans wanted. To believe.

"Indians" were what Europeans believed.

"Indians were what Europeans believed."

Believe it or not.
Believe it or not.
Believe it or not.
Believe it or not!
Believe it or not!

Believing the Belief

They believed!
Oh my, yes, they believed!
Soon, very quickly, there were Indians!

If it's one thing Europeans knew how to do, it was to believe!
They still do, you won't believe it even though it's true!

Oh, their belief in the power of belief is powerful!

Their power to believe was beyond belief!
It was overwhelming!
They believed, they believed!

Soon the Americans believed
since they were originally Europeans
and they yearned for "the old country."
Oh my, they believed!
They absolutely believed!

Even "the Indians" Believed

Indians were made up?

Yeah.

They became what people in Europe believed them to be? Indians?

Indians.

Indians?

Yeah, Indians.

Soon there were Indians all over the place. But mainly in the New World, especially in America! Indians thrived in the New World. That's where they were seen the most. That's where they "belonged." That's where they were the most Indian!

> Soon even "the Indians" believed there were "Indians."
> Soon even the "Indians" believed they were Indians.

Nonetheless they were people.
They were hanoh. They were people who were themselves.
They were people who were their own people.

> See Indians.
> See real Indians.
> See real Indians play.
> See real Indians work.

> But there was nothing to see.
> There was nothing.
> Because there was nothing there.
> Nothing real
> or surreal.
> To see.

See real Indians.
Where?
Where?

Where.
No where.

Wнат Wе Кпоw

So where were the Indians?
What did Europeans see?
Did they see anything?
What did they see?
Did they see people?
Did they see people like themselves?
What did they see?

What did they see?
What did they see.
What did they see.

"Indians" who are our people

(The People, Human Beings, Hanoh, etc.)

knew themselves as people. Different from each other. Speaking

different and distinct and separate languages. They heard each others'

languages. Their people had different names. They wore different

clothes. They ate different foods. They danced different dances. They

celebrated their differences. Yes, they were different but they were all
the same:
The People, Human Beings, You, Me.

Always just Like You just Like Me

Meanwhile
and meantime
and always

After and before
and during
and always

always no matter what always and always and even despite
the greatest believers and disbelievers in the world, they/we were people
they/we were/are people we/they are people four times and without
number or need for number we/they are people just like you and just
like me

PART THREE

Gifts

To Plant Again

Sometimes I take a walk to the garden we used to have.

All of us, the kids and everyone, would work together on it.
Getting the spring ground ready, clearing away the winter weeds,
planting seeds, waiting for new plants to come up, irrigating them,
making sure weeds didn't take over, always talking as we worked.

We would always have a good lunch, it would be like a picnic.
There was always lots of laughing and joking going on I remember.
At their gardens other families also like ours would be nearby.
And we would wave to each other when we and they arrived.

In the 1960's my sons went into the United States Army. Japan,
Thailand, Puerto Rico. I planted our garden by myself, irrigated,
chopped weeds. Corn, chili, carrots, beets, onions, some cilantro.
Sometimes my grandkids helped, and I'd tell them of years before.

I'm older now these days. These present years are good and bad,
just like they were back then. I feel good about what is possible.
Sometimes I take a walk to the garden we will come to plant again.

Your Eternity

More than all the years,
hard work, events, comings and goings,
and all the successes and failures,
joyous and sad times,
it's this moment of family,
friends, admirers, comforters,
and others,
              this is all your own, a gift
of loving and caring and courage
and patience.

A Picture

I want to show you a picture which is the story in this poem.

Twenty years or so ago my mother said this.

"My little sister and I stood with this one old woman
when the men and boys left Acoma to look for work in California.
Kaalrrahuul-rree-neeyaatse 'tseh eku.
The Acoma people had gathered at the plaza to watch them leave.
And to give them all their love and prayers.
A few of them had horses and some had burros
but most of them amoo-uh were on foot.
It was a very poor time then. I think it was 1910 or 1911.
All the people were having a hard time. It was a sad time that time.
They had to leave Acoma to make a living, to look for work for pay.
And all that time since then I remember a song
the men and boys were singing when they left.

Kaalrrahuul-rree-neeyaa-ah
Kaalrrahuul-rree-neeyaa-ah
Kaalrrahuul-rree-neeyaa-ah
Kaalrrahuul-rree-neeyaa-ah

Kaalrrahuul-rree-neeyaa-ah
Kaalrrahuul-rree-neeyah-ah-ah
Shteh-eh-yuu-uuh.

That evening my sister and I stood by ourselves
at the western edge of the Acoma mesa.
Red clouds were in the sky. I remember saying it was dust
rising from the feet of the men and boys walking
as they looked for work in California."

And so twenty years later this is the picture I am showing you.

Califor-ni-ya-aa
Califor-ni-ya-aa
Califor-ni-ya-aa
Califor-ni-ya-aa

Califor-ni-ya-aa
Califor-ni-ya-aa-ah
Let us go-oh.

A Gift to Give and Receive

A tribute for the children, April 1994,
Charlotte, North Carolina

Let your hands fall open.
Let light fall upon your palms.
Hold the light in your hands.
You are holding light in the palms of your hands.

This morning I look in the flower pot
hanging from the back porch support beam.
The buds of the plants are just now coming into blossom.
This season's white petals with reddish-pink stems.
Days ago when I returned to Pembroke
I noticed a bird fly away from the pot.
And opening the porch door this morning I saw it again.
So standing on my toes, holding for balance
to the wooden porch railing I look
for what I thought was there.

And there it was, a sparrow's nest
which could easily fit into the palm of my hand.
Amidst the stems of a spring plant, there it was.
A delicate web of tiny sticks,
thin dry leaves and grass, and downy feathers.
And there they were, five delicate eggs
smaller than the tips of my little fingers.
There they were, off-white shells speckled with blue,
there they were.

Only looking on then
and feeling a wonder and an awe,
I knew I must let them be
the fragile and delicate life they were.
Within this April's light, we are sheltered and joined.

Balancing on my toes, holding to the porch railing,
I could only be filled with my wonder and my awe.

There is a delicate and fragile world all around us.
Even now, even as this morning is aglow
with spring light on new wheat and sorghum fields,
tall slender trees, and nearby Lumbee homes.
Even now, even as I am filled with a wonder and an awe.
It is a delicate and fragile world we do not often see
but there it is and there we are.
Like the sparrow's nest and the sparrow's eggs
in the flower pot out back, a delicate and fragile balance
of life and ever continuing life.

Hold your hand open.
It is the light you hold.
Hold your heart open.
It is the world you hold.

If I were to reach into the flower pot
I could easily lift away the sparrow's nest and eggs
since they would fit into my hand.
Because the nest and eggs are that small,
that accessible, they are that easy to disturb.
For a moment then, only a fleeting moment,
I would know the tiny quiver of the sparrow's life.
I would know. And I would know I was to have let it be.

Hold out your hand then and into it let the light fall.
Accept this, this simple gift.
And then into the palm of another's hand
let this light, this same light, fall.
And know it is the same light the sparrow
and its care and love gives and receives.
And know it is the same light human parents
and their care and love give and receive.
And know it is the same light human children

and their care and love give and receive.
Feel the light given and feel the light received.
Feel the light received and feel the light given.
This is the gift.
This is the gift.
It is yours to receive and give.
It is ours to give and receive.

Their Gift

64

Delighted to show us,
Daniel Lorenzo dances
the motion of his fat little fingers.
Although not yet three years old,
he knows the gift of his breath
and what it is to be within
his presence as a child.

Krista Rae has this knowledge too,
absolutely certain of the smiling glow
and light she holds toward us, her kin,
who are delighted by her as she senses
the wonderful presence of our love
gently surging among ourselves.

This is the gift of their childhood
offered openly because it is everything
they have, and we are awed by how worthy
they make us feel to receive such a gift.
How precious it is to open ourselves
to moments of our own simplicity
and to savor simpler knowledge once more.

Epic

Mythic roads lead us beyond ourselves.
It doesn't matter where they lead.
We are there on them heading beyond.
They could be returning or leaving.
We could be leaving or returning.

TELLING AND SHOWING HER

For Stah-ma-ahka Sara Marie

Duwah ya-aie dzah. This is the dirt.
Duwah haatse dzah. This is the land.

Duwah sra-ah. This is ours.
Duwah sra-ah haatse. This is our land.

How-nu chuutah. Reach down to it.
Pihtya ya-aie. Touch the dirt.
Pihtya haatse. Touch the land.

Dyuu tchu-u-tah ya-aie. Pick up the dirt.
Dyuu tchah-yow-uuh haatse. Pick up the land.

Ya-aie sru-taie-kquiyah. Dirt you are holding.
Haatse sru-taie-kquiyah. Land you are carrying.

You are holding your life. You are carrying your life.
This is what I am showing and telling you.
This is what I am telling and showing you.

Sparrows

in the fireworks
of dill blooming
like roots of light

that shall never be seen again

seen once and always

sparrows with us

once and forever

.

Our Children Will Not Be Afraid

For Ihtsatyanee, Stah-ma-ahka

It will at last be the children's, their own destiny—
the weapons of their spirits, their souls
shall surge forth with an honest anger and grief
that will not be kept within them.

But be driven, as ever it was, a hope
that is not forsaken since it was not ever defenseless.
Yes, it will thrive not broken nor poor-spirited
but courageous with destiny and strong with history.

O shall they, the thieves and killers and liars, endeavor
to overcome us but will and shall fail. Let their madness
be their mark; let them fail on their own not from our fears.
O let them. Let us not flail ourselves upon their illusions.

Let us not be too urgent; these things take time.
Let us raise our children to be wonderful
and healthy, wise and determined against injustice.
O let us not waste the precious moments we have.

Our call is for a life that will bring us health,
a strong and continuing health that wields its spirit
against those who steal our precious mark
upon the sacred stone and store of our land.

Marking my own stricken yet struggling word, I owe something
to this Earth Our Mother. Let my debt be without loss;
let it be with song, joyous, affirmed, loving.
For the reason is I am alive, you are alive, we are alive!

Sing forth then, let all hear from the depths
of our hungry bones and the marrow that will not dry.

Let us sing then, let us be lovingly decisive before it is late.
Let us not be consumed by despair that is not ours.

Our children will welcome the call and song into their breasts.
Their dreams will be engendered by Popée, Tecumseh, Crazy Horse,
Chief Joseph, Geronimo, and all our grandmothers and grandfathers.
And they will hear them say their lives are our lives, their hearts our
hearts.
And they will come to know it will not be the thieves, killers, liars
but our people who will have victory!

FOR THE CHILDREN

> They say the children were "traded"
> for the bells at Mission de San Estevan
> after the battle at Acoma in 1599 when
> the Conquistadores were the victors.

The children were taken.
To the south they were taken.
And they never returned.

Many years later
from the south, bells for the mission were brought.
They say the Kashtuurlah Rey sent the bells.
He sent them for the children
who were "traded" to the south.
The bells were for the children
who would never return.

In the south wall
of the wall around the graveyard, there is a hole.
The round hole is small but it is big enough
for a little boy or a little girl to climb through.
They say it is for the Aacqumeh children
who were taken away, who were taken away.

It is a door, the round hole, for the children
to climb through when they return,
when they return to Acoma one day.

Still today the people wait.

Always the Song

For Jim Pepper, brother-friend, who died February 10, 1992

Just recently I've been trying to remember my dreams, Jim. Too often I've not
bothered to recall them, even arrogantly thinking they were irrelevant, thinking
I didn't have to recall them. But now lately I've said to myself I must remember
my dreams.

I was waiting and I had been waiting for a while.
It was early morning, very early, and it was still dark
but there were brilliant distant stars that early morning.
The night before there had been a new moon in the west.
And now at its crescent edge, there was an aura of light.

I was at the woodpile, the old woodpile when I was a boy.
Nearby thirty yards away was my boyhood home where
in this time-place of the early morning past and present
my mother and other family members were fast asleep.
I had just come out of a small adobe cabin where I lived
and I sat down on an upended piñon log at the woodpile.
All around was a gentle odor of juniper and piñon wood
and kindling in the cool air of the season of the dream.

I was waiting but I didn't actually know why I was waiting.
But I felt good about it and I was patient and peaceful.
I was relaxed and watchful in the early, early morning.
Above and all around was the huge, limitless dark sky.
There was no definite season apparent, nothing at all,
but it was comfortable and I was content to be waiting.

Then just as I turned my head eastward looking to see
if the dawnlight was soon to be showing on the horizon,
I heard noises coming toward me from the southwest.
Someone was coming out of the early morning dark,
approaching the woodpile where I was sitting on the log.

My attention was drawn to two men who greeted me,
hailing me hello, laughing softly, speaking familiarly
and warmly.

Looking closely at them and squinting my eyes,
I recognized Jim Pepper who smiled that boyish, open,
teasing smile of his, and I instantly felt joyful to hear
his murmuring laughter, and I waved my hand at him.

I didn't move from the piñon log I was sitting on
as I watched Jim begin to unpack his saxophone.
The other musician, a guitarist friend of his
began to tune up also getting ready to play.
Looking over at me as he fixed his mouthpiece,
Jim said something which I didn't quite hear
and he laughed softly aloud as I nodded my head.
Yes, yes I meant. Yes, I want to hear your music.
Nothing would make me happier than to hear the music
you share with your soul, heart, and spirit I nodded.

When he and the guitarist began to play their music
I did worry momentarily about how loud it might be
because of my relatives sleeping in the house nearby.
However, after looking toward the eastern horizon
and seeing the approaching dawn, I decided yes,
how wonderful it would be for the world to wake up
to the soaring eagle flight music of Jim Pepper.
And I remembered the song that came to me years ago
as part of the story of Wren who is just a little bird
when he was told his song was for the awakening
of All Creation!
Yes, yes, I motioned with my hands,
it is wonderful to awaken in the morning
with the rest of All Creation.

And the song of the Eagle and the Wren and the song
of all the myriad and wondrous beings and items of life

whirled all around as Jim's breath became an exaltation
of the song of our souls, hearts, and spirits.

The song surrounded me in the world of that dawn.
It wove me into the universe of mountains, plains,
oceans, skies, galaxies all around, all the plant
and animal world we know and don't know.
It took my life into a dimension not mine anymore
but was the song of a world that could only belong
to Earth the Mother which is the Creation
and Existence of All Things.

                    Ever so powerfully
the music was urgent and yet soothing and soaring
like I've always known Jim Pepper's music to be,
ever so insistent for the world to awaken and go forth.
Always the song that is the Earth's and Ours will urge us
to help each other and to be together on this our journey.

On the early morning of that recent dream I was happy and grateful to wake
   up to a song that called upon all life to go forth into the light of the world
   that was now the dawn. Thank you, I said softly. Thank you, Jim, for the
   song of the dawn this morning.

Rain

Bill and I stand in the rain smoking.
A Gypsy from Romania joins us.

Bill and I talk about the Portland Powwow.
The Gypsy asks, "What's a powwow?"

Bill says, "It's a celebration.
Indian people dance and sing for life."

The Gypsy says, "It's not a talk?
Like Bush and Gorbachev? They come
to an agreement in their powwow."

"We agree to celebrate," I say.

It's been raining for days.
It's going to keep raining for days.

Bill says, "It's a religious event.
People get together to sing and dance."

The Gypsy says, "Do Indians believe
the Mormons? They say Indians
are a lost tribe of Jews."

"Mormons say a lot of things," I say.

Then the Gypsy says, "White men killed
the Indians in the east and the west.
It's in their nature to kill."

Bill asks the Gypsy from Romania,
"What do the Gypsies believe?"

The Gypsy looks away and doesn't answer.

The rain keeps falling; it will rain
for days and days and more days.

Thinking aloud I say, "Probably
like Indians, the old religion of Gypsies
was a belief in the creation of all things
and the holiness of sky, land, and people."

To the things I say, the Gypsy says, "No."
His voice is very quiet, and he looks away.

Bill and I both look at the Gypsy.

"The rain," I say, feeling the constant rain.
Today the rain cannot be denied at all.

"No," the Gypsy says, and he looks at Bill.

And then looks at me and Bill, and he asks,
"How did you Indian guys make it?"

Waiting for a Friend

It's their business what they do
obviously.
               But I'm a worrier.
And maybe it's that I don't want to see
myself either, that's what I hear
in the back of my mind.
                         Nevertheless
I feel the concern.

                         I know the loss
of lost things, the falling sound
in the dark, the subtle and vague quake
I've never known what to do with.

Where he could be I don't know.
He, Eugene, called last night and though
I don't know him well, only met him
recently, I worry about him.
The streets, the dark, his age,
the foolish frailty I know too well.
It's the madness that fools us,
the shared yearning for the whiskey,
light dry white wine, whatever.
                         It's that.

It's pretty women and blue and sad song
I've sought. The yearning they hold for me.
It's the countless tricks I've relied on,
the skill I've managed to lose things by.
It's myself I worry about obviously.

Eugene knows himself well enough
what the long dark holds.
                         He knows Henry,

Berryman's standby, waiting just offstage,
just around the next corner, only a half step
away to turn into shadow or the light.

We know the history of self-exile.
We have begged ourselves too often
not to know the truth.
                        We know no standby
can fill in for us, instead would only
fail us again, never let us enter
or exit properly even though it's over.

I won't wait this time even in pain.
                        It's awful
how honest we have to be in truth at last.

The Laughing Horse

Remembering Ed Dorn, poet and storyteller. And a laughing horse, of course.

A poet with a laughing horse came to town one day in the early 1970s and told us stories at the local bookstore. A man telling us he couldn't be anything if he wasn't always riding trails of tribulation and trial and trouble, and adventure too, always unforeseen but always ready. And his laughing horse? Yes, yes, of course, his horse. Cautious, wise, and nimble, he was. And clever. What would a cowboy be without a horse. Yes, yes, of course, but a horse that laughed? Well, yes, what would a horse be without a laugh! And just think of it, what would a poet and his story be without a horse that laughed?!!

That's why my four-year-old son who is now a thirty-one-year-old lawyer laughed and laughed along with the poet and his laughing horse. Of course!

PART FOUR

Horizons

Not Knowing and Knowing

"I don't know how Wild Horse Island was lost,"
Julie says, looking wistfully across the lake.
"I don't know what happened."
Waiting for my prime rib dinner
at KwaTaqNuk Resort at Flathead Bay,
I want to agree with her.
I want to say I don't know either.

This morning talking with two young friends.
Both of them skinny, one Lakota, one Tsalagi.
Both of them trying so hard to raise their boys.
Both of them trying so hard to finish school.
They tell me things about living in Missoula.

"Where are all the Indians in this town?" I ask.
After first looking at each other they say,
"Down at the Mission, down the street."

Now I sit looking out at the spectacular view.
Mission Mountains, their flanks facing Flathead Lake,
the sun, shifting shadows, the lake shimmering
burnished silver, beauty unmatched, unmatched.

Along the large bay windows sit white people
dining, occupied with harmless chitchat it seems.
I don't see any of them look at the lake at all.
They look too prominent and successful to notice.

And maybe they are harmless after all, I think, and maybe
just maybe, if I ask politely enough they would tell me—
if they know—just how Wild Horse Island was lost.

By the time my prime rib dinner arrives
my hand that picks up the steak knife is trembling.

Cutting into the meat, I feel weak and confused,
and I want to get up immediately and leave.

But I do not leave. I sit looking across the lake
knowing the very same answer Julie knows.
Knowing there is no other answer but the one
Julie knows after all. I do not leave; I cannot. I stay
bound by the absolute and loving beauty of this land.

More than anything else
what we want to feel and finally know is the prairie's song.
With this cored tightly always and forever enduring in ourselves,
we can know
all manners and dimensions of grief and we will not fail ourselves.
Today such a song pushing bitterly yet beautifully is about.
A winter chant biting into skin, hair, and bone as fiercely as any starving
teeth
ever did.
Yet it holds us faithfully; nothing can separate us.
It is a cold knife between skin and bone, the senses and the mind, the
physical
and the metaphysical, and there is nothing to do but to know it,
lean into it, smile
tightly.
It is to live after all that is our answer to the death-pushers; it is our
victory.
Nothing can ever remind us to live so much as now;
this more than anything else is our song, the prairie's song.

This is our poor prayer; it is despair
we realize; and how we hold our eyes
hidden yet holding them out, appealing,
our memory instinctive and true.
We're always in danger, expectant even
that our fear will rip the peaceful air,
pushing the question toward the edge
into too much silence and disbelief.
It is then that we should prefer
the most common bond offering itself;
this has always been, this is ours
more than destiny—it is death, the life
in the winter air, the prairie that is horizon,
the instinct that is not fearful, hungry, alone.

It is our shoulders then that carry us
as they have always done, proudly,
innately joyful, dignified, and humble.
And though this prayer is despair momentarily
it is not dark and pushed aside as loss.
This prayer is not hidden but chanted
and certain as the prairie's song.

Blue Whale, the Largest Living Animal I've Never Seen

I've never seen one except on a
postcard, and I know no postcard
is large enough for life.

I didn't see this blue whale on exhibit
at the American Museum of Natural History.
I just bought a postcard, but I was just thinking.

This animal is the largest animal in the world.
Maybe it's so large we don't see it.
It's so big it overwhelms our comprehension,
throws our usual senses out of kilter.

On the postcard is the blue whale upside down
or are we and the room upside down?

The whale is so huge we can only accept it
for what it is, sacred and alive,
powerfully taking us beyond the Museum
into the beauty and sacred that creation is.

Kaweshtima Sharing Its Existence with Me and Me Sharing My Existence with Kaweshtima

Looking North seeing Kaweshtima,
the strong mountain is a prayer.

On cold winter days, the Mountain
is tall, huge, strong, and sacred.
On hot summer days, the Mountain
is sharp, clear, and forever.

On all days of Creation's seasons
there is always clarity.
It occurs to me again
that wherever I have been
I have never seen another Mountain
which has stood more clearly
in my mind and heart.

When I have needed to envision
my home, land, family,
when loneliness for myself
has overcome me,
the Mountain has occurred.

And now it prays its being with me.
And now I share my being with it.

Look to the Mountain

Always, it shall be this way.
Always, it shall be this way.
Always, it shall be this way.
Always, it shall be this way.

Tee-dyameeh
Buu-nahmeeh
Koo-wahmeeh
Haa-nahmeeh.

To the North
To the West
To the South
To the East.

Tee-dyameeh
aishtuh Quutih guh-chahnih.
Buu-nahmeeh
aishtuh Quutih guh-chahnih.
Koo-wahmeeh
aishtuh Quutih guh-chahnih.
Haa-nahmeeh
aishtuh Quutih guh-chahnih.

To the North
a Mountain is standing.
To the West
a Mountain is standing.
To the South
a Mountain is standing.
To the East
a Mountain is standing.

All around in all the sacred directions of the Earth
a Mountain is standing. Look!
And look from all the sacred directions of the Earth
we are standing here. Look!

Look to the Mountain.
Look from the Mountain.
Look all around and within.
Look within and all around.

In thankfulness, we see the Mountain.
In thankfulness, we see from the Mountain.
In thankfulness, we are standing with the Mountain.
In thankfulness, we are standing with each other.
Look to the Mountain, we are standing with the Mountain.
Look from the Mountain, we are standing with each other.

Always it shall be this way.
Always it shall be this way.
Always it shall be this way.
Always it shall be this way.

Mountains All Around

Driving up Grant, she hollers,
Where are we going?
I look at her and say,
Home for me and you're off to work.
And then she laughs and says,
My car was headed home.

All around the sacred mountains
that enclose Tucson, all around.
Whenever I need to locate myself
I look for the mountains I know.
It doesn't matter where I am
I look for mountains I know.

North, West, South, East, all around,
they are the horizon we're within.

Kuutra Tsah-tseh-ma Srutai-kyuiyah

Duwah ya-aie dzah.
Duwah haatse dzah.

Duwah sra-ah.
Duwah sra-ah haatse.

How-nu chuutah.
Pihtya ya-aie.
Pihtya haatse.

Dyuu tchu-uh-tah ya-aie.
Dyuu tcha-yow-uuh haatse.

Ya-aie sru-taie-kqui-yah.
Haatse sru-taie-kqui-yah.

Kuutra tsah-tseh-mah sru-taikyuiyah.
Duwaah ehme hau shrauyuu pehni eh sraupeh tah.
Duwaah ehme sraupeh tah eh hau srauyuu pehni.

Your Life You Are Carrying

This is the dirt
This is the land.

This is ours.
This is our land.

Reach down.
Touch the dirt.
Touch the land.

Pick up the dirt.
Pick up the land.

Dirt you are holding.
Land you are carrying.

Your life you are carrying.
This is what I am showing and telling you.
This is what I am telling and showing you.

Da-aah Mehyuu-nah Nuudeh-guyah Sru'tsah

Steh-gaadzeh yukeh kaatyah-stih nuwaakameh-eh sru'tsah.
Nieukah-chana sru'tsah, guwaa unah-kaatyah srahanu tyiemeeshi
   dzeh-ehmishee,
guwaa dzieu-kai-ih-tishii, guwaa sramee-dzeh-ehmeeshi.

Duweh waitsih hanu stutah-ah-tehsi, emeh eh nyieu-kai-ih sru-tsah.
Ehmih eh heyah sramee eh dawaa eh niwautra-skuwaadrumah.

Keemuu ehmih eh yuuni ganaatah'tsi:
Dawaah eh aneh eh, dawaah eh aneh eh dzah.
Tuu dyuutrusrah dawaah eh aneh eh, nu daa guh.

This Is the Way Still We Shall Go On

It is necessary to look back to the past.
Gazing we will see how our peoples in the past lived,
how they were guided, how they lived well.

We who are living today, that is what we are to be guided by.
That is the way of living that will be correct and good for us.

As you know that is what the song says:
Good and beautiful, good and beautiful it is.
Always it will be good and beautiful, it will be.

Aнmoo Staiyatru-tyaimishi, Da-aн Srai-tru-nih

Dyaamih He-shuunih
Kah-chahni
Ih'tsatyahni
Kaweshtima
Kah-chahni K'yuuni
Srakaiyah
Shuutih Muuti

'Tsahmuuti
'Tsahmaa-akah
'Tsahmaa-akah
'Tsabaabah
'Tsabaabah
'Tsabaabah
'Tsanaanah

Ha-ah, duwah tsai howbah staiyahtrutyaimishi tsah-ah, ahmoo-uh.

Beloved My Descendants, I Know You This Way

Eagle Prayer Feather
Rainy
Precious Stonebead Pin
Snow Covered Female Mountain
Rainy's Song
Srakaiyah
Wren Boy

My son
My daughter
My daughter
My granddaughter

My granddaughter
My granddaughter
My grandson

Yes, these are all my descendants, they are, beloved.

Hihdruutsi, Nuyuuh Da-ah-sheeya 'Tsadzehni Neeya Emeh-eh-eh'tseh

Hihdruutsi. Dyaamih Hanu 'tsudah.
Aacqu 'tsau-uh.
Aacqumeh Hanu 'tsudah.
Ehmeh eh shruweh 'tsayuukai.
'Tsa-dze kuwaah ihska-nudaaskuunuh.
Nu-wah dumeetra kudruu'tsah srahmih.
Ehmeh eh shruweh neeweeh tahwaanah dumah'tsah.

Dze-dyuuka chaanah-tyuu hatih yuunah dihtyah, bunami, kuwami,
   hanami,
ehmeh eh neeweeh tahwaanah dumah'tsah.
Nu 'tranah kudruu'tsah: Wah kuumeh Hihdruutsi.
Muu eh haitah kaanahtrutyaiyah?
Muu ehmi dyowskee'tsih?

Shruweh nuhtranah kuudruu'tsa:
Guwaadze, Hihdruutsi!
Gai-trudruuskeetsih?

Ha-ah, ehmeh eh da-ah neeweeh tawanah duumahtsah.

Hihdruutsi, In the Way of My Own Language That Is My Name

Hihdruutsi. I am of the Eagle People.
Aacqu is my home.
I am of the Acoma people.
That is the way therefore I regard myself.
I cannot be any other way or person.
You must learn this well.
That is the way therefore you will recognize me.

When you see me somewhere to the north, west, south, east,
that is the way you will recognize me.
You will say: Why that is Hihdruutsi!

I wonder where he has been traveling at?
I wonder if he has been well?

And then you will say:
How are you, Hihdruutsi!
Have you been well?

Yes, that is the way then you will recognize me.

Dᴢᴀʜ-ᴅᴢᴇпᴀʜ Hᴀᴍᴀᴀ'ᴛᴢᴇʜ-sʜɪᴍᴇʜ-пᴀʜ Kᴜᴜs'ɢᴀɪʏᴜᴜпᴜʜ

Hah-ah, kaimah'tse, dzah-dzenah wai ehmeh-nah eh-eh dzeh shruunu.
Mahmeh, kuuyah kgu.
Yuu-gaikah hamah, dzadze chu'sgaiyuunuh.
Yuu-gaikah hamah, dzadze ehmeh dah nu.
Yuu-gaikah hamah, dzadze guwah eeska ti-ieutu nimah tyanuh.
Sra hanu tyaimishi nuyuh kowyugaiyeeshi neeya deh-eh.
Ehmeh gai-kah yu dah.

Shruweh guuwah wai, neetra nah shru'tsah?
Yuutah-ah truwah 'tsih-teesh-tah.

Tsee-meh-yuunah nuu-deh-eh shru'tsah.
'Dseh gaa-dzeh.
Hahtru-tsai-meh.
Kuu-meh.
Tsah-dze guuwah eeska neetrah-nah sgu-tsah tyanu.

Hah-ah, tuyumah dzah-dzenah hamaa'tzeh'shi meh-nah 'tsah-nu,
'dseh gaa-dzeh, meh yuunu yaani nuwaakameh eh shru'tsah.
Eh-meh eh mehyuunah nu'deh-guyah sru'tsah.

İᴛ İs пᴏ Lᴏпɢᴇʀ ᴛʜᴇ Sᴀᴍᴇ ᴀs İᴛ Wᴀs ɪп ᴛʜᴇ Oʟᴅᴇп Dᴀʏs

Yes, it's true, it is no longer today the same.
Very much, it has changed.
In the past, it was not different.
In the past, it was not that way.
In the past, we did not have another way of knowing.
Our people only by their own way of seeing lived.
This was the way it used to be.

How and what is it today we shall do?
This is the way you must be thinking.

98

We must continue to be.
It is necessary.
With courage (as men).
With courage (as women).
There is no other way different that we shall do.

Yes, although it is no longer like the past days were,
still necessarily toward the future we must look.
That is the way still we must keep on going.

LAND AND STARS, THE ONLY KNOWLEDGE

North, West, South, and East.
Above and Below and All Around.
Within knowledge of the land,
we are existent.
Within knowledge of the stars,
we are existent.

Coldness and wind and the snow, northward.
Mildness and mountain and the rain, westward.
Hotness and desert and the hail, southward.
Warmness and mesa and the sun, eastward.
Starshine and sky and the darkness, upward.
Earthsource and stone and the light, downward.

By this Northern Mountain, we live.
On this Western Peak, we live.
In this Southern Canyon, we live.
Upon this Eastern Mesa, we live.
Below this Sky Above, we live.
Above this Earth Below, we live.

We are Existent within knowledge of land.
We are Existent within knowledge of stars.
All Around and Below and Above.
East, South, West, and North.
This is our prayer. This is our knowledge.
This is our source. This is our existence.

Always the land is with us.
Always the stars are with us.
With our hands, we know the sacred earth.
With our spirits, we know the sacred sky.
We are with the land and stars.
We are with the stars and land.

With offering, all around outside.
With offering, all around inside.
This is the knowledge we have.
100 This is the existence we have.
In thankfulness, we give and we know.
In thankfulness, we receive and we know.

Beauty All Around: A Moment on the Lakota Prairie

Now the sun is so low on the horizon.
Now there is a rainbow circled all around the sun.
Now there are three suns, one is in the center.
Now there is beauty all around.

The song-prayer must be for this.

Looking eastward, just above the hills at mid-morning,
circle around the center is immense, shimmering
in rainbow colors, the circle complete,
its bottom arc at our feet, and standing before it
we are within the sphere.

> In beauty before me.
> In beauty above me.
> In beauty below me.
> In beauty all around me.

Nothing but the totality of the sun
and winter snow and being alive and knowing
it could be nothing more than beauty.

This is the song and the prayer.

What is it we do when we borrow? Here in this poem, I use *hozhoni*, a
Diné concept. Beauty all around. Hozhoni. Beauty everywhere. All beauty.
Spelling this concept as a word that sounds sort of like the Diné word.
Using sounds of the English language alphabet. How correct, accurate,
and appropriate is it? I don't know. Close or not close? Sort of close I
think. Close enough to sound. Writing out sounds of language using one
language's written script for another is a poor way to represent spoken
language. Yet that's all we have. Do we? For now. Unless we come up
with another way. So we borrow. I guess that's what we're doing. When
I use the English language, am I borrowing? Or using what's available?

Yes, using what's there. Because it's available and possible. So I borrow in a sense but mainly because I'm using what is at hand. When I do that— using what's at hand—I'm not really borrowing though. It's using the language I'm within at the moment, a language of feeling and thought, a language in which I'm a presence, a language that I'm a presence within, a language therefore that gives me presence. Something like that. So when I feel and think within hozhoni, I am within hozhoni and that is my presence.

Getting Ready

Split piñon and cottonwood logs this morning.
See Lloyd taking the stones out of the pit.
Watch Jesse bring the wheelbarrow over.
Split some more piñon logs.

    We are here.
    The blue mountains are over there.
    Lloyd asks, "What are those
    mountains called?"
    "Sangre de Cristo," I tell him.

Call to James to help Jesse.
See Jesse limping back to the sweat lodge.
See James K. start to lay logs for the stones.
Think I've split enough wood.

    We are everywhere.
    The acts of Creation are everywhere.
    Stone, wood, fire, and water.
    These are the elements.

Walk to the fire pit and help.
Wad up newspapers and push them between logs.
Study the wind a moment and light the paper.
Hope the fire will catch quickly.

    We have only this place.
    It's always been like this.
    One time, one place at once.
    Nothing but ourselves, the nearby mountains,

our voices, our preparation to become.

Culture and the Universe

Two nights ago
in the canyon darkness,
only the half-moon and stars,
only mere men.
Prayer, faith, love,
existence.
                    We are measured
by vastness beyond ourselves.
Dark is light.
Stone is rising.

I don't know
if humankind understands
culture: the act
of being human
is not easy knowledge.

With painted wooden sticks
and feathers, we journey
into the canyon toward stone,
a massive presence
in midwinter.

We stop.
                    Lean into me.
                    The universe
sings in quiet meditation.

We are wordless:
                    I am in you.

Without knowing why
culture needs our knowledge,
we are one self in the canyon.

And the stone wall

I lean upon spins me
wordless and silent
to the reach of stars
and to the heavens within.

It's not humankind after all
nor is it culture
that limits us.
It is the vastness
we do not enter.
It is the stars
we do not let own us.

Making Quiltwork

Like the coat of many colors, the letters, scraps,
all those odds and bits we live by, we have come
to know. Folks here live by the pretty quilts
they make, more than make actually, more than pretty.
They are histories, their lives and their quilts.
Indian people who have been scattered, sundered
into odds and bits, determined to remake whole cloth.
Nothing quits. It changes many times, sometimes
to something we don't want, but we again gather
the pieces, study them, decide, make decisions again,
yes, and fit them to color, necessity, conditions,
taste and choice, and start again. Our lives are quilts,
letters, odds and bits, scraps, but always the thread
loving through them, the compassionate knowledge
that what we make is worth it and will outlast
anything that was before and will be worthy
of any people's art, endeavor, and final triumph.

Here, look at my clothes, quilts, coats of many colors!

More Than Just a River

A river is more than just a river.

I grew up alongside the *chunah*—the Rio de San Jose—which emerges from beneath the volcanic lava beds west of Deetseyaamah (or McCartys, in English), a farming village north of Aacqu, the old pueblo. As Acoma people we have always believed the chunah (our Acoma name for it, which denotes the natural landscape feature of a watercourse or channel) was more than just a water source. It was more than just irrigation water for our corn, chili, and alfalfa fields, more than just water for our households and for our livestock, and more than just a great native trout-fishing stream I knew as a boy. It was a life-giving force coming eastward from Hee-shamih Quuti in the Zuni Mountains to the west and the Continental Divide of which the mountains are a part, and the water in the chunah followed the same route the Shiwana did when they, as rain clouds, brought their sacred life-giving moisture to us.

A river is more than just a river.

You would think you can't learn to swim in a little stream of water that was sometimes no more than three inches deep. But I did, because where the chunah turned southward just east of Molinaa-tsih and below the Ray and Sanchez places, it was deeper, maybe four feet deep since the river was sort of dammed at that spot. And you wouldn't think the chunah was where you committed your first acts of "sabotage" against the state when you and your younger brothers "freed" the native trout the State Game and Fishery people caught in wire-mesh traps to take elsewhere and transplant. And you wouldn't think the chunah was where you remembered what your big sister Rachel said was important when you got in a fight— "Don't cry"—although in the fight with Danny, which I lost, it was hard not to cry.

A river is more than just a river.

One hunting season when I was sixteen years old after I brought a big buck home with me from hunting in the Zuni Mountains, a commemorative thank-you dinner was held for the deer. All our Eagle clan relatives came, everyone admired the huge rack of antlers on the deer's head in a big cooking pot on the kitchen stove and ate the good venison boiled with corn, pinto beans, and piñon nuts, and many of them kept asking the hunters for stories about the hunt. Before the deer dinner guests left for their homes with covered bowls of deer stew, a woman who is *stah-kuuya* spoke prayer words of blessings and good wishes. As an elder of my father's Antelope clan of which I am their child, she wished me courage and health, blessed me with appreciation for providing food for our people, and urged upon me an abundance of male virility always. And then stah-kuuya "ate" the deer's eyes!—which meant she removed them from the deer's head and would take them to the chunah where she would pray with them. So the deer would return always to the source of continuing life; so the river would always help us to return life to continuing life.

A river is more than just a river.

I was maybe four years of age when I attempted to cross over the chunah by myself for the first time. My mother and I were going after our horses Charley and Bill which were grazing on the other side of the river. As we approached the shaky pine board which served as a bridge across the river, my mother took my little hand in hers and said, "Hold my hand tightly. Just hold on, son. Don't let go." Making sure my hand was securely held in hers, cautiously we stepped onto the plank board and began to make our way over the chunah. At that place the water in the chunah was not so deep nor flowed very fast, but to a little boy it was deep and strong and fast enough! Yet because "I was a big boy" who did not need his mother to hold his hand, I said, "I can cross the chunah by myself. I can do it!" and I assertively took my hand from my mother's hand. Though very hesitant and uncertain, my mother said, "All right, son. Just go slow and be very careful," and let me go on my own. Halfway across the chunah, the unsteady bridge began to tremble and sway and the boy who thought he could cross over by himself fell into the cold water with a big splash. And crying, "Ahmoo, stamuutih," my beloved mother who always believed I could cross over whatever I needed to jumped right into the chunah and rescued me!

A river is more than just a river.

Sometimes it's kind of hard to explain "Indian things" to non-Indian people. On the reservation when I was in grade school, all the teachers were white people. One day some of our sixth-grade classmates were not in school. When the teacher called the class roll and almost all of the boys were not there to say "Here" when their names were called, she asked why they were not in school. None of the rest of us sixth graders uttered a single word. There was suddenly an unexplainable silence in the room, and I'm sure all of us students wore very blank faces. Then the teacher asked again, "Why are the boys not here?" Her loud and demanding voice made us nervous and even more silent. There was an uncomfortable quiet until one of the girls from the back of the classroom quietly said, "Chi-sheh kah-owpahsranee-ih." "What did you say?!" the teacher said, "Speak louder. In English." Looking down at her desk, the girl would not say anything more. Then in English, another student said, "They went to chase the Apaches to fight them." "What!" the teacher exclaimed, this time even louder. "Chasing Apaches? Acomas don't fight Apaches anymore!" But that's what the boys were doing, participating in a traditional ritual experience known as Chisheh uupahsranee-ih that occurs when boys will soon reach maturity. They are taken by elders to an area where the chunah waters gather in lava ponds, and there with prayer, advice, and story the boys are told their land, culture, and community must always be helped and protected by them.

A river is more than just a river.

Acoma elders always talked about days of long ago when the grass would grow as high as horses' bellies because it would rain and rain and lightning would dance and leap from mountain to mesa to mountain and thunder would roll out of the canyons unto the valley of Aacqu and the fields and pastures of Deetseyaamah. As a boy I would listen avidly because, according to those stories, the olden days were lush with good weather and had a future that seemed to be nothing less than propitious. I felt somewhat unfortunate about my own days since the summers I knew were mostly rainless and hot and the grass grew barely a few inches above the dry dusty ground, and we were always wishing for rain. Or wishing that we lived in the tropics where it really rained! However, I recall at least two times when the river rose because it rained and rained. What a wondrous sight to behold actually! Days of thunderstorms in the Zuni Mountains to the west and the San Mateo Mountains to the north and Srakaiyah Quuti to the south caused rainwaters to flood into the chunah until its riverbanks overflowed and the little river expanded into a shining sea that seemed to flow for miles and miles! Seeing the river at flood stage, smelling its ripe and fertile odor, that was what it felt like to me. A sea! Except for those times, I've never seen the chunah like that. So when I am older perhaps I, too, like those elders I listened to when I was a boy, will speak about the time when it rained and rained and rained and the chunah turned into a sea!

Yes, a river is more than just a river.

I live in Tucson now, and except for an El Niño season several years ago which actually made the desert land pretty wondrous and even lush it doesn't rain much there. So when I come to New Mexico, I always look forward to seeing the Rio Grande—Tsihchu Chunah it would be called in the Acoma language, or Big River—at Hatch. There the river, which I'm always happy to see, is a shining dark swath through the Hatch valley with its verdant acres of chili, corn, alfalfa, orchards, and pasture lands. I return to the river always with a prayer of thankfulness because I know that the chunah of Rio de San Jose that I knew in my Acoma childhood flows eastward as a tributary and eventually becomes a part of the Rio Grande. And I know that when I come to the Tsihchu Chunah and follow it upriver, I will be following more than just my memories of the river I knew. And when I arrive at home I will be assured that memory is more than just a memory, just like a river is more than just a river.

Yes, a river is more than just a river.

PART FIVE

EVER

Consternation

Consternation may be the moon
that was full days ago, I don't know.
The tilt not proven enough, its glimmer
of light off cant some, an odd angle.
Leverage of mountain range, a soaring
silver coastline, the southern gale
too early in the autumn, untimely.

Things result from causes my part
in the celestial motion has no bearing on.
I don't know the surge overcoming me,
a sudden spilling of tears no one sees
nor why my final marrow is desperate.

Growing up certain with knowledge
and firm in belief in the Milky Way
and farther constellations no moment
was ever doubtful; this knowledge was more
than a mere rendering of the mortal mind:
it was shown plain as lines on the palm
that was plain as a map of the universe.
Of this there was never any doubt.

Until the moon full and a night beyond
inexorably pushed the enormous foundry
of the earth's core beyond its limits.
Even within the concave of my skull
my eyeballs tremored,
                    aware of a tumult of tugs
                          only ancient children know.
I ache now with a shaking that doesn't stop yet.
There is doubt now. I know it deliberately.
Yet I'm always tied to the constellation;
the concavity of the constellation presses

upon the sphere of my eye; there is no way
to cease this consternation.

On the night before the moon was last full
I told the woman I have loved for two decades
that I loved her still; I told her again I mean.
I've not been mistaken in my final belief
it is essential to believe we have to do
with the heavens; of that I have no doubt.
The news of gales and earthquakes in California
will not deter us from the journeys we take
through this reality the only heaven we know.
Not mistaken in this belief and faith and love,
we can accept this consternation.

In El Paso Many Birthdays Ago

> "Maggie of a thousand summers"
> —notebook journal entry, original source unknown, recalled
> and copied from the elsewhere world of youth

It's like centuries ago now, although as I recall
I was twenty then, solitary, pensive, at odds
with the U.S. Army, family, college, and too serious.
Already drinking too much, writing in El Paso bars,
having metaphysical debates with myself, falling
in love.
        On that birthday, a Saturday, I ached
to be remembered in just that sad way only youth
and self-absorption knows needing it for who knows
exactly why.
        She sat down beside me, a lonely soldier
from Fort Bliss, and picked up one of my paperbacks,
Walt Whitman or Ezra Pound or whatever, and before
I could stop her she grabbed my notebook and read
a poem I had just written.

The poem doesn't matter now, many words, many years
later, but centuries ago then
                  I see her turning to me,
laughing warmly, putting my hand in hers, telling me
with her eyes it doesn't really matter how fiercely
we hold our innocence against loss nor hold our youth
against the years.
        What matters is the present one,
the time today we are to hold forever and precious.

That birthday poem written for that day, for that shy
awkward boy now becomes a quiet acknowledgment,
a loving present I've learned to accept and give away.
And Maggie, lost innocence and lost years many days
and summers ago, is still precious and forever that day.

Tsegi Canyon

Motel
at the edge of stone
deep sigh.

It may be the last.

Stone above canyon.

Wind music.
We try to find the words.

Stone hot afternoon
between Kayenta
and Tuba City.

It will not be the last
place, words, or motel.

By the Cottonwood

not much for the day

just blue blue desert sky
and the rillito which i've longed
and longed and longed

and longed once again

to show you
to tell you about

i feel sand in my sandals
i feel the grains gritty between my toes

i wish you well
well i wish you more than well

from here in the desert riverbed
where i came to renew myself
after i left you in santa fe

all my love
all my love
however way that can help you
now
all my love

a prayer whisper wish

Hunting for Stones

On the shore of Flathead Lake

Just little things.
Irregular little things.

I want to hold these

        precious

   as they are

      memories

         perhaps

but perhaps more than that.

I don't know.
Maybe I've known.
Maybe I will never know.

Agate you said.
        I said they were accumulations
of pitch—tree sap—petrified.

And you looked at me, studying
me, discovering again
me, a person uttering surmises.

And I think I only smiled.
Because I really don't know much of anything.

Except I do know we are

        aggregates

and accumulations also.

And that is precious,

                        not perhaps

but precious.

No Weather Map

Poems are not weather reports.
No data, no radar pictures. Yet
somehow my sense of things
and the way I map my way requires
a clear design that I can look at.
So in the morning I look outside
or sometimes in mid-afternoon,
and there it is a climate of air,
wind, sun, much rain, such quirkiness
sometimes I just don't know what.
It's poetry I end up with, image
I behold and believe, a fine slant
of sunlight suddenly appearing
at treetop or the long vast days
of rain and more rain and the river
squalls coming up the Willamette
from the Columbia and the Coast.
Nothing stops this poetic data
in its purest form. Thin boundaries
of the coastal range nor the wishes
I dare make for hours of sunshine.
My weather is in the living margin
open to me, the place where I stand
and the place I see; this is poetry
and the design my journey needs.

Kite

Ocean Isle, North Carolina, March 1994

We left the kite unflown.
Left it still in its plastic sheath.
Just like it'd come to the gas station
from Taiwan. Or from Japan.
Maybe Florida? New York?
We didn't let it fly after all.

Seagulls, the tide coming in, later
going out, the pier in the distance.
He wanted to remember everything.
But a week later, he couldn't.

What can you say when you say good-bye?
Maybe after all there is no good way.
I have to read your letter again.
What can I say when I don't wish good-bye?
And just want to hold and hold.

When they stood on the trembling pier
he looked out to the ocean horizon, searching.
For what he didn't know, and then sought
for something bearable and enough.
It's okay he thought, it's bearable and enough.

A kite tumbles in the wind, a butterfly.
It dances too soon across a wintry meadow.
The butterfly's freedom doesn't know.
Why it dances, why it's tossed by the wind.

We don't even know the wind may change
sooner than we know from cold to colder.

But even then, he wished they had freed the kite
from its plastic sheath and let it dance.

But even then, I wish they had freed the kite
from its plastic sheath and let it dance.

But even then, I wish we had freed that kite
from its plastic sheath and let it dance.

And watched it sail toward a horizon that was ours.

What I Know

Things don't always have to be on the edge.
I have a choice. The edge is not just right there.
It is away from me. I am away from it.

Twenty years ago in South Carolina
I'm walking on the beach I tell Kelly.
But I don't know whether the sun is rising
in the east or in the west this morning.
I'm cold and hungry but I think it's rising
or falling.
          I still don't know sometimes.

Yesterday morning the rainy wind dragged
wet leaves across the parking lots of Portland.
And the dim sun spun gray edges around curbs,
street signs, tree trunks, city buildings.

How we see is not always a test
and we don't really know all real things.
Wet leaves, cold wind, bus engine roar,
and sunlight.
          Spinning, rising, or falling
is real, and when the edge is there or here
and I'm still nearing or drawing away from it
this is my choice. This is what I know.

Light

Out to mail a letter at the corner mailbox,
morning moment, the sunlight caught
me striding loosely uphill. I cannot mistake
this morning for what it is: sunshine, air
quick and rich in spirit, alert in my eye.
It is here; I'm crystallized for a moment,
light gleaming at a hill bottom. But it's only
Broderick and Haight, a California city.
It's the power of the solar cosmos holding
me upon the rent tortured covering of self,
making me a patchwork; this is my redemption
after all this morning; this is what will fly me
with the posted mail more than words, more
than language, a swift incision that opens me.
Light, light, the sun's force sears me cleanly
with the joy of the hilly park above me. I
cannot deny light's eager touch, opening petals
of my flowering heart, the sparkling cells
sharing the simple and deeply joyous laughter
of my voice which opens like a child's. Ho!
Light of this morning, I am alive, alive with you.

February and Violet

Two days after Valentine's Day
the intermittent rain still falls.
Or is it snow? Days, weeks, months
of bone and muscle tightness, tension
of holding little warmth to body.
This morning though I look outside
and right out there beyond the ledge
are tulips. Maybe those are not them
but they're something starting with violet
petals. Perhaps they're the color purple?
What their name is in this precious now
is my discovery, the significant act
I need—rain or snow, tulips or what,
yesterday or tomorrow—and for this
I am alive! Intermittent desires, gain
and loss, warmth and wishes fleeting
will still be here more than momentary,
even eternal, but the moment of seeing,
looking outside and just right there
always will be the discovery offered me.

Thin, thin metal
shrieking,
sheet tin or wire
against other metal.
And wind cold,
uneasy, resentful, loose,
a weak raging.

What can I be
but human, a husk
of too much mind
and only a shred
of emotion?

I want the bird to be a bird,
wind to be wind,
cold to be cold,
me to be me.
And unfretful,
not at edges
too close, so very close.

When I speak with a friend
on the telephone she tells me of illness,
an imbalance of time and work and body,
and I do not know what to say
except give my best wishes for health,
offer advice for rest, to let go.

We deserve health, rest, letting go.
We deserve to know the bird is a bird,
illness is illness, edges are edges,
and ourselves to be ourselves.

Pause: Yours: Ours

"Just pausing," she writes from Wyoming.

We're on opposite sides of the Continental Divide.

Yet I could be on her side. And she could be on this side.

Pause before the next step. "Or leap."

We're not butterflies though we may wish to be.
      Though we may imagine to be.
            Though we may become aflight at times.

A pause is never absolute or too wide or fearful or minor.

The pause is there as it should be.
      Significant, special, a moment to savor.
            A space to let yourself be held within.
                  A space and moment that is.

Admitting

Cleo, it was so good to see you.

I was surprised, even shocked.
Months it's been, and more than that.
Time and circumstance remove us,
doesn't give us the one more chance
we selfishly, selfishly want.
It's all right we think; it's okay.
That's mostly what I need to say.

After the alcoholics meeting we go
to the hospital, to the pharmacy.
Medication and the shit
one goes through to survive.
We talk of how hard it is
to face our need for help.
It's so easy to turn away, turn
to something else, so damn easy.
I ask what crosstops are.
Although I know what they are.
Speed, Cleo says, street speed.
How we turn deftly from ourselves.

Walking into the hospital
I am afraid she will fall.
I feel tremendously helpless,
and admitting powerlessness
does not help at all this time.
We cannot bear to fall limp,
collapse onto the dirty floor.
What we can't stand we face though.
I make ready to catch her.
It is for this I make preparation,
and even the inevitability I wait for.

Cleo and I make it though as usual.
Actually I'm in a cold sweat.
I twitter nervously, mince my steps
and my words, and she has to laugh.
I feel love precariously but easily
and this time I know compassion
for us, our weakness, a natural
collapse we have to admit to.
This is what we're all prone to, nothing
more than our need for humble strength
and sacred courage, a cry for help.

Eagle Wing

Partners at seventy the generations

More than change or time
We are here with each other
Before one another always

Always another one before
Other each with here are we
Time or change than more

Partners at seventy the generations

Flagstaff Notes

Hummingbird comes by singing a hummingbird song.

My heart leaps into song. Leaps into a hummingbird song.

This morning Thea and I jog and walk up the mountain to a meadow.

See two fallen-down pine trees, old, rotting, split.

And a house of logs too at the edge of the meadow.

North of the mountain are patches of snow. Older and recent snow.

Clouds moving, clouds moving, air alternating from warm to cool.

We plan to pick wildflowers. Yellow, blue, white. For Peg.

But we take another road. And do not pick wildflowers.

We always seem to take another road. The heart leaps and leaps on its
  own trail.

Hummingbird's song. Follow me says the song, follow me.

(Sunday, May 31, 1986)

FEBRUARY 7, 1998

Now it's almost twelve years later. Whoa! Time passes. We don't know
why or how, but it does! Now Thea is at Stanford. Twelve years ago she
was eight or nine years old. On our walk that day we didn't pick mountain
flowers for her mother Peg. Time and things happening and time passing.
Whoa! That's what we want to do sometimes. Stop it. Stop time. Time.
But we don't. We can't. Time is not something we're really really really
aware of although "it" is happening all the time! Like floating through

space with no reference points. Like traveling between mountain peaks as if we levitate somehow from one point to another point across a space of space that has no real and actual reference points. Except for not picking yellow, blue, and white wildflowers. Except for such things, we don't remember time. Times passes. And we pass through time.

PART SIX

CONNECTIONS AFTER ALL

Beginning and Ending Song

part 1

Yes, you Honor, Judge.
Yes, you Honor, Judge.
Yes, you Honor, Judge.
You Honor, you Honor, Judge.

Now I ask you, Judge.
Now I ask you, Judge.
Now I ask you, Judge.
I ask you now, Judge.

Where's my land, Judge?
Where's my land, Judge?
Where's my land, Judge?
Where is my land, Judge?

Where's my life, Judge?
Where's my life, Judge?
Where's my life, Judge?
Where is my life, Judge?

Where's my land, Judge?
Where's my life, Judge?
Where's my land, Judge?
Where is my life, Judge?

Where is my life, Judge?

Пothinɢ but Eterɲity

March 4, 1994

"Nh . . . kiss."

A child's voice halts.
On the telephone.
Question, distance, distance.
This moment is eternal.
My answering hello stopped
                        short,
                        faltering.

Finally my silence broken
with my repeated hello. Hello?
Hello. And another, this time gently
                        urgent.
Until I have to say, "Let me talk
to your momma."

Then a brief space of quiet
on the line is made more eternal
by my unspoken questions,
the horizons I've tried
and failed to reach.

And too much distance

                    until

there is nothing but silence.
Then beep, beep, beep, beep.

Speechless, I have to hang up,
breaking the connection.

Not daring to move I hold the phone in my heavy hand, look at the black
plastic piece, wait for it to tell me something. Anything. Something I
crucially need to know.

Nothing. Nothing. There is only an eternity of silence holding me.

Busted Boy

He couldn't have been more than sixteen years old,
likely even fifteen. Skinny black teenager, loose sweater.
When I got on Bus #6 at Prince and 1st Avenue,
he got on too and took a seat across from me.
A kid I didn't notice too much because two older guys,
street pros reeking with wine, started talking to me.
They were going to California, get their welfare checks,
then come back to Arizona in time for food stamps.

When the bus pulled into Ronstadt Transit Center,
the kid was the last to get off the bus right behind me.
I started to cross the street to wait for Bus #8
when two burly men, one in a neat leather jacket
and the other in a sweat shirt, both cool yet stern,
smoothly grabbed the kid and backed him against
a streetlight pole and quickly cuffed him to the pole.

Plastic handcuffs. Practiced manner. Efficiently done.
Along with another Indian, I watch what's happening.
Nobody seems to notice or they don't really want to see.
Everything is quiet and normal, nothing's disturbed.
The other Indian and I exchange glances, nod, turn away.
Busted boy. Busted Indians. Busted lives. Busted again.

I look around for the street guys going to California.
But they're already gone, headed for the railroad tracks.
I'm new in Tucson but I'm not a stranger to this scene.
Waiting for the bus, I don't look around for plainclothes.
I know they're there, in this America, waiting. There; here.
Waiting for busted boys, busted Indians, busted lives.

Meanwhile: Soon the Millennia: Burning Forests: Indians Killed: October 6, 1997

What a strange time it is.

Princess Diana dies. (Not even sure if she's a real princess although stupidly she is called the people's princess.)

Then Mother Teresa dies. In honor of Diana. (?) Maybe to appease God, maybe to apologize.

Then Ted Turner gives a billion dollars (sort of) to the UN. With strings. To "inspire" (?) other billionaires. He says. Yeah right. And Turner reports (chortles) Jane cried with joy when he told her about his gift. Yeah right.

Then Bob Dylan sings for the Pope. Where's the skinny 1960s junky? Where's the Polish priest? And soon the Pope heads for Brazil. (Where Indians are still dying, still dying, still dying. Still getting killed.)

Meanwhile.

The forests are burning in Indonesia.

Meanwhile.

The forests are burning in the Amazon.

Meanwhile.

U.S. Attorney General Reno says Vice President Gore will be sacrificed in order to save the presidency. And now he will never be president.

(That's throwing out the bathwater with the baby. That's killing the baby to save the man. Or is it the other way around? Or killing the Indian to save the man? Or what is it when it's not a moral dilemma?)

Meanwhile.

People do not know how horrible it's going to be when the Republicans win the presidency the next time. Not different, just how horrible it will be. How much more horrible. Shudder. And quake. And people will think it's because of the millennium.

Soon. It's time. Soon.

I hear the Rolling Stones are playing the Oakland Coliseum. Mick Jagger's picture was in the newspaper. He looks like a monkey, Marilyn says. Same thing. All I saw was Mick Jagger reborn as Mick Jagger. Same thing.

Meanwhile.

Merle Haggard and Willie Nelson sing on *Austin City Limits*. They look like old white men on TV. Because they are.

Same thing.

And the forests are burning. They're all burning. Indonesia is burning down, Indira says.

Soon the U.S. will send a $3.4 billion plutonium-powered Casini spacecraft to Saturn to check on its eighteen moons. On October 13. Good thing it's not a Friday. But it is a Monday.

Soon.

Does Saturn have forests to burn like the Amazon, like Indonesia, like Oregon and Idaho and Montana? Don't worry, it's safe: President Clinton approves. Both the U.S. stock market and the world economy are strong and vigorous. What a miracle; it's not Friday; thank God.

But soon. Like now.

(And the Indians keep getting killed, keep losing land in the Amazon, in Brazil, in Indonesia, in Washington, D.C., soon on Saturn.)

God will not accept Mother T's apology.

Meanwhile. And soon.

The forests are burning, burning, burning, burning. Smell the smoke.

Like now.

Mutant and Wise

child
          of colonialism

strange

          but not so strange

but true

and too true

the human mind is a curious trap

what i like is what i want to be

the distant thunder

                    in the distance
                              coming closer

close

close

enough to know the blue mountains

from where it came

in the graywhite mist

around everywhere

around everywhere

the distance

is within

is not without

but is the thunder rolling into itself

over and over and over again

like always

over and over and over again

rolling into you

rolling into me

rolling into you

rolling from the sky from the mountains from the distance into you into
   me over and
over again

i am a stone in the desert

waiting and waiting and waiting for the rain that will come

knowing it will come waiting for it to come

knowing it will come hearing it from beyond

waiting waiting waiting let the thunder roll and roll from the horizon
   rolling toward me

toward you toward me toward you

and

waiting

144

　　　　　stones that's what we are

　　　　　　　　　　　waiting for the thunder the coming and
coming and coming

Past Poems

Where are the Indians in this crummy town?

My temptation is to go up to the first white man I see
and say, "Where are all the Indians in your crummy town?"

One of the hills overlooking Missoula has a big white M painted on it.
And another hill not far away has a big L.

Once in a poem I wrote there were Indians everywhere.
Maybe I was wrong. Maybe it isn't true.

In another poem in another crummy town I wrote
"I just want to climb that hill, cross the next river,
go through that clump of trees, and see the earth new again"
or something like that. But a good poem.

Maybe I was wrong.

An older white man at the corner of Higgins & Main mumbles
incoherently and hollers very loudly, "Burn!"

"Burn!" Very loudly. Then more incoherent mumbles.
And then "Burn!" even more loudly, in fact, yelling this time.

When I walk by him close to the curb I see he has a worn Bible
clutched tightly in a skinny hand held at his side.
His other hand waving weakly seems detached somehow.

I find myself trembling with a mix of fear, compassion, love.

Love? And compassion? Yes. And I know I was not wrong.

Looking past a tall bank building I see the hillsides again.
They're there, painted with the *M* and the *L*, they're there.

A poem I wrote called "Claiming Territory" says it was easy
to cross prairie hills, see all that land, proclaim "This is mine!"
The prairies and rivers did not say anything.
The mountains and hills did not say anything.
Everything was astounded and quieted in dismay.

Earlier that day on my way from the airport to the hotel,
the airport van driver said, "You see new stuff everywhere.
Everywhere you look new construction is going on."

I wonder about that Wisconsin Horse standing quietly
looking through the chain-link fence watching
and watching America building something else.

That was just a poem I tell myself; it was just a poem.

Later, on my walk back to the hotel in Missoula, I don't see
the white man with the Bible who was yelling "Burn" loudly
and strangely I miss his stark avenging presence.

"Why?" I ask myself. And answer myself: He's the man
who would have told me where all the Indians were.

The Best Movies

I've always loved good movies.
It's that the best ones always make me look
inside, look at places and things I don't always notice,
places and things I deny, where I think things aren't.
It's those places that need to be seen and the movies,
the best ones, make me know them again.

It has to do with realizing our lives
are not simply dust and fluff
but real and solid, even the empty moments.
We can see them on the screen because
the best ones don't flinch away.
In fact they make sure we catch ourselves
in the moments when we're looking away.

I don't know; I've never tried to write
about why I've always loved the movies.
It's an old love, knowing and accepting
there are truths that someone else
points out to me from time to time.
And I can say, Ah ha, yes, this and more
is how a story is told and facing it
is a major part of the story that is mine.

Time as Memory as Story

Let's say it's half a century later.
Let's say it's never too late.
Let's say Skull Valley.
Let's say.

Time has no mercy. It's there. It stays still or it moves.
And you're there with it. Staying still or moving with it.
I think it moves. And we move with it. And keep moving.

Eleven years old and soon to be in fifth grade. That's time.
Boys' time. Who knows what time is but them. Eternally.
No one knows time better than they. Always and forever.

Our family. Mama, me, Angie, Gilbert, Earl, Louise.
Kids. Daddy working in Skull Valley for the AT&SF RY.
Mama just packed us up in New Mexico and moved us.

Suddenly. A surprise. To me anyway. To join Daddy.
Who was away most of the time. Arizona. California.
Sometimes Colorado. Sometimes Texas. Always away.

Railroad work, labor, heavy machinery. Rails and sun.
Trains always moving. I remember the war. The 1940s.
Soldiers. Tanks. Cannons with huge guns and wheels.

Time does have mercy. But it doesn't enumerate or wait.
It moves. And we move with it. Though for boys, maybe?
I wanted it to wait. So things could happen more gently.

A boy misses his father. A boy watches younger sisters.
And younger brothers. All growing. And he's growing.
And he misses the times his mother is happy, laughing.

Who knows time as well as boys and their young worries?
I was a boy growing within family, community. And dreams.
And girls. Girl teenagers. I adored them, their pretty ways.

In the fourth grade at McCartys. Made a bookshelf in shop.
Proudly. Sanded. Varnished. Shiny. For my Mama.
With love. I wanted to be a good carpenter like my Dad.

Dad drank though. Dark moods. Dark scary times. Danger.
And words hurtful, abrasive, accusing. Anger, pain, scorn.
A boy wonders. About time. About forever. When it ends.

I loved my Dad. Wonderful. Skilled man. Artist, singer.
Precious and assuring. Yet. Yet. Unpredictable moments.
You can never tell about time either. Like that, it is. It is.

We farmed. Corn, melons, chili, beets, carrots, cilantro.
Onions. Even potatoes in little mounds but they died.
Corn fields at night. Irrigating. June nights. I loved forever.

My grandpa I loved very much. Time was soothing then.
We didn't really need time when days and nights were safe.
And with him they were. A healer and respected kiva elder.

Herded his sheep. Along with my uncle Estevan. And Roy.
Roy was a strange one. Chinese manner. So people said.
From Chinatown in California. He had a gentle soft smile.

And a storyteller he was. Yes. About his horse. Lightning.
Fast and nimble and quick. Lightning, his horse. He'd ride.
Yes, ride to see his girl to call her outside. Estella! Estella!

Stories. I'd listen. The boy I was. Seeing my uncle riding.
Riding his fast and nimble horse. I'd listen and he'd smile.
Memory and time. It doesn't count all the time. Listening.

And because mothers are always loving. Alert. Ever caring.
Mama decided we must go to Skull Valley where Dad was.
Up to Grants, the depot there, we got on the westbound train.

Sacks and boxes, a trunk, suitcase or two. Clothes, things.
What did we have? I don't remember. Not much though.
We never had much. Poor. And lonely for Dad always away.

I wonder. I wonder. Too often that's been the Indian story.
Father gone. Mother and kids left behind. Is it like that?
Yes, too much. Dad didn't like working for the hard railroad.

He'd complain and rant about the crude and mean whites.
The slave rules. The company. Trains powerful, unending.
Time I thought was in the trains. Fast, loud, dangerous.

I was afraid of the powerful trains. Like I said I'd see them.
Soldiers, army troop trains, going east and going west.
Unending. I wondered where they were all going. Where?

Lightning and thunder trapped in the train power and steel.
Yet I yearned for blue song. Hollow and lonely long tone.
Coming round the bend, and something beyond the horizon.

Far away maybe. Travel. Some other dream. Youth. Yes.
I liked songs. Music I heard on the radio. Hank Williams.
And stories that rang through the air. Talk and listening.

It was the first time ever we were leaving the reservation.
Only one world till then it seemed. Acoma community. Ours.
On the edge of another world though, something strange.

And fearful too. The dark moments. Like when Daddy drank.
When there was fire from another world. An unknown.
Yet fascinating somehow, oddly, something on the far horizon.

I didn't remember riding the train before. Ever! Until then.
Like riding thunder. The horse, Lightning, Roy talked about.
Riding off somewhere into the dark night. Fast, fast. Fast.

Riding toward night. We watched the land speeding away.
Far across the land, along the edge of it was a highway.
With cars and trucks. Moving, moving. Only slower.

Time speeds, like you speed. Only not an awareness.
Or any way to tell what is taking place. When young.
And you're trying to furnish your own answers, solutions.

To mysteries you're anxious about. When all's uncertain.
Youth is not the time when time is apparent. Too slow.
Or too fast. And you don't really have clear reasons. Yet.

At Ashfork we got off the train onto the depot platform.
I sensed being lost. Lost mother and lost children. Dusk.
Where was this world? Where did home go? Children?

Lost at the edge of a strange world with a gray green depot.
Large letters painted. Little sister is hungry. She whimpers.
Mama says, "Hold my hand." We walk, up street, walk, walk.

It could be Indians. A family, mother and children. Lost?
Where are they going? Up the street I think. Looking.
For something to eat. My mother held only a little money.

Hamburgers we split. Water and water. Self-conscious.
Moment is time. I looked out and saw a train passing.
Our train! I thought it was our train. But it wasn't, just fear!

Wait. Then a train down Chino Valley. Long-distance night.
Stars vanished in too much night. Long day into night.
Where does time go? Does it go nowhere but into night?

Then at the sudden edge. The horizon. A vast bowl of light.
And only at the far end, trees. And still far ahead of us.
The train engine light. Always a light showing the way.

My brother and I excited. A deer stunned by train light.
Stilled. Stark. A cut stone. The dazzling moment held us.
Youth and time. Nothing like it. Thrilled. Never until then.

Years later I tried to tell about that moment to a love.
But love is time too. So. Can't do anything but live time.
The horizon and beyond. Full of stars. Even unseen.

Always belief is firmer than faith. With and without dreams.
We arrived in Skull Valley early in the morning. Three-thirty?
Where were we? On the other side of the moon from Acoma.

A mother and her children and assorted bags and boxes.
Dreams. Time. Horizon. Farther from home than belief.
It felt like that. Within moment when you can't turn away.

A train depot on the other side of the moon. Deserted.
After the train pulled away. Only the rails and starshine.
What's a boy say to his mother? Earlier than anything.

A man whose picture I'd seen. White man. With a cap.
With a visor. Sitting at a tall wooden desk with shelves.
And a metal puzzle thing making clicking-clacking noises.

Who spoke with Mama. Who smiled. Who wondered at us.
An Indian woman with Indian children. Who were strangers.
Like we just came from the planet Acoma. The other side.

Of day. Of the present early morning night in that moment.
The telegrapher with the visor said. I think. I think he did.
He knew my father. Knew where he lived. Two miles away.

So we took a road. Early, early morning night trek. Time.
Shimmers in an odd amazing way. Within what might be.
A boy and story. The dawn coming. Horizon ever so near.

When we knocked on his railroad worker housing door.
Daddy was shocked. In his underwear. Shadows upon.
And the background of his and Mama's and our history.

We come to discover each other. All failures and gains.
Counting and mattering, no matter the time or sequence.
We laugh and hug and cry. Daddy. Daddy. We're here.

Once again together. Family, history, travel, time, love.
To say what time is, even fifty years in the past to now.
In this moment, Skull Valley is just as real as it ever was.

Memory we cross and cross again. Treks, trauma, and on.
We do know what time is. It is loss and gain. A lingering.
Within discovery we come to ourselves. Finding. Destiny.

Moments recalled like friends. It was that way or another.
We're fairly certain either way. Stories. They are with us.
Time doesn't forsake. It doesn't soothe or decrease. Never.

Skull Valley. A time for a boy. History engulfed beyond.
When I went back. Recently. I ate with friends at the cafe.
By the railroad tracks. I was fascinated by photographs.

Of the mountain lions in the mountains nearby. Ever there.
No matter what. And the stories of bones. Tall tales or truths.
They're told. Apaches, it's said. Wagon trains. Lies or no.

Our history is more than here. We know more than realize.
We realize what we don't know. Or want to know. Truths.
Stalk us, just like they found. A boy. More than fifty years ago.

He discovered a world beyond Acoma. A world apart.
And a world together as time, memory, as story. As his own.
We seek and are found. Secure. Actual. Safe. And serene.

154

Last summer near Prescott that boy fifty vast years later.
Found carved images on stone walls that fit his hands.
Carved in time. Eternal as stone. Past and present. Ever.

Let's say it is ever an ongoing story.

Just Call It Smiling for Victory

At the Federal Building, Albuquerque

Everybody is smiling.
Lena hands me a baby in her cradleboard.
"A warrior," I say.
"She's a girl," Lena says.
"Yes, a warrior," I say.
Everybody is smiling.

Don't anybody ever tell you that Indians never smile.
Don't anybody ever tell you that Indians never win.

Everybody is smiling.
The baby's father is holding her.
"What's her name?" I ask.
He tells me and adds,
"She was born at home, Big Mountain."
Her father smiles.
"Big Mountain Woman," I say.
Everybody is smiling.

Don't anybody ever tell you that you're not right.
Don't anybody ever tell you that it is all in vain.

For you are the people.
For you are the people of this land.
For you are the warriors.
For you are the voices.
For you are the smiles
of a human spirit that will win.
For you are the smiles of victory.

Don't anybody ever tell you that you're not right.
Don't anybody ever tell you that Indians never win.

Don't anybody ever tell you that it is all in vain.
Don't anybody ever tell you that Indians never smile.

Just look at all those smiles!

BEGINNING AND ENDING SONG

PARt 2

Fifty days jail.
Fifty days jail.
Fifty days jail.
You say I'll stay and pay, Judge.

Fifty dollar fine.
Fifty dollar fine.
Fifty dollar fine.
You say I'll pay or stay, Judge.

You say I'll pay, Judge.
You say I'll pay, Judge.
You say I'll pay, Judge.
You say I'll pay or stay, Judge.

You say I'll pay or stay, Judge.

No, I say, Judge.
No, I say, Judge.
No, I say, Judge.
No way I'll pay or stay, Judge.

No, I say, Judge.
No, I say, Judge.
No, I say, Judge.
No way I'll stay or pay, Judge.

Yes, you Honor, Judge.
Yes, you Honor, Judge.
Yes, you Honor, Judge.
You honor no honor, Judge.

Yes, Your Honor, Judge.
Yes, Your Honor, Judge.
Yes, Your Honor, Judge.
You honor no honor, Judge.

You honor no honor, Judge.

About the Author

Simon J. Ortiz is an Indigenous poet, fiction writer, essayist, and storyteller. He is a native of Acoma Pueblo in New Mexico, where he grew up at Deetseyaamah, a rural village area in the Acoma Pueblo community. He is the father of three children—Raho, Rainy, and Sara—and is a grandfather. As a major Native writer, he insists on telling the story of his people's land, culture, and community, a story marred by the social, political, economic, and cultural conflicts with Euro-American society. Ortiz's insistence, however, is upon a story that stresses vision and hope by creative struggle and resistance against human and technological oppression. His works include *The Good Rainbow Road*, *Men on the Moon*, *from Sand Creek*, *Speaking for the Generations*, *After and Before the Lightning*, *Woven Stone*, *The People Shall Continue*, and *Earth Power Coming*. He has received award recognition from the National Endowment for the Arts, Lila Wallace-Reader's Digest Fund Awards, Lannan Foundation's Artists in Residence, "Returning the Gift" Lifetime Achievement Award, WESTAF Lifetime Achievement Award, and the New Mexico Governor's Award for Excellence in Art. He lives in Tempe, Arizona, where he is a professor at Arizona State University. At ASU, he coordinates the Indigenous Speakers Series, which bi-annually hosts the Simon Ortiz and Labriola Center Lecture on Indigenous Land, Culture, and Community.